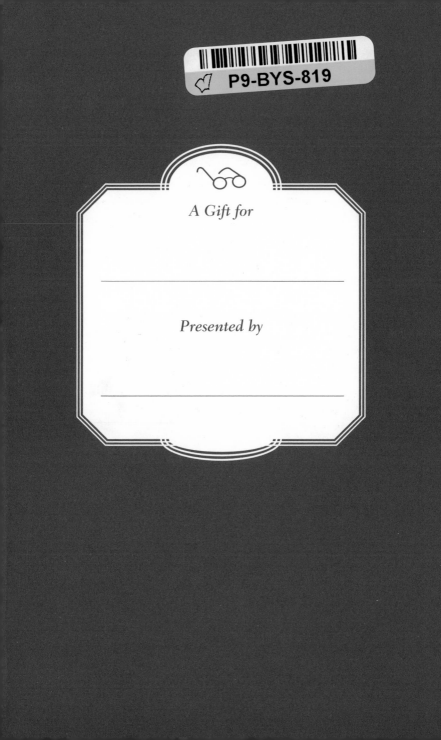

A Gift for

_____

Presented by

_____

My Grammar and I...
Or Should
That Be "Me"?

My Grammar and I...
Or Should
That Be "Me"?

*How to Speak
and Write It Right*

CAROLINE TAGGART
J. A. WINES

Reader's
Digest

The Reader's Digest Association
Pleasantville, NY / Montreal

A READER'S DIGEST BOOK

Copyright © 2009 Michael O'Mara Books Limited

Reader's Digest is a registered trademark of
The Reader's Digest Association, Inc.

First published in Great Britain in 2008 by Michael O'Mara Books
Limited, 9 Lion Yard, Tremadoc Road, London SW4 7NQ

FOR READER'S DIGEST

U.S. Project Editors: Sarah Janssen, Abigail Wilentz

Copy Editor: Siobhan Sullivan

Canadian Project Editor: Pamela Johnson

Project Production Coordinator: Wayne Morrison

Senior Art Director: George McKeon

Executive Editor, Trade Publishing: Dolores York

Manufacturing Manager: Elizabeth Dinda

Associate Publisher: Rosanne McManus

President and Publisher, Trade Publishing: Harold Clarke

Taggart, Caroline
  My grammar and I ... or should that be "me"? : how to speak and write it right /
Caroline Taggart, J.A. Wines.
     p. cm.
  ISBN 978-1-60652-026-0
  1. English language--Grammar--Miscellanea. I. Wines, J. A. II. Title.

PE1112.T34 2009
428.2--dc22

2009015349

We are committed to both the quality of our products and the service we provide
to our customers. We value your comments, so please feel free to contact us.

The Reader's Digest Association, Inc.
Adult Trade Publishing
Reader's Digest Road
Pleasantville, NY 10570-7000

For more Reader's Digest products and information, visit our website:

www.rd.com (in the United States)

www.readersdigest.ca (in Canada)

Printed in the United States of America

7 9 10 8 6

English usage is sometimes more than mere taste, judgment, and education—sometimes it's sheer luck, like getting across the street.

—E. B. WHITE

CONTENTS

INTRODUCTION

It is in the nature of a living language to evolve, since new inventions require new words, foreign influences enliven the vocabulary, and social changes give people more or less leisure to write at length. The monks who copied out medieval texts invented short forms to save themselves time, which passed into the language as ligatures in words such as *mediæval*, which we now deem archaic. In our own time great revolutions have occurred because of e-mailing and texting, and who knows: a standard dictionary of 2028 may well contain the word *gr8* (great).

We cannot stop English from changing—and only the most ardent, dyed-in-the-wool pedants waste their time trying—but we can do our best to ensure that it does not become compromised along the way, and to preserve its best features. Since linguistic sloppiness often leads to ambiguity—one of the things that grammar rules try to avoid—a few rules are surely a good thing. And frankly, if you can't bring yourself to agree with that, you might as well stop reading now and get your money back before the book starts to look tattered.

Rules were very much in the minds of the sticklers of the eighteenth century, who, fearing for the health of the English language, decided to impose on it a grammar system that would fix it "good and proper." Unfortunately for us, these scholars were specialists in ancient Greek and Latin—not German, the language from which English is derived—so they imposed a number of Latin rules that didn't fit too comfortably with English, thereby creating all manner of unnecessary complications.

GRAMMAR RULES (TO AVOID)

1. Verbs has to agree with their subjects.
2. Remember to never split an infinitive.
3. Parenthetical remarks (however relevant) are (usually) unnecessary.
4. Never use a big word when a diminutive one would suffice.
5. Use words correctly, irregardless of how others elude to them.
6. Use the apostrophe in it's proper place and omit it when its not needed.
7. Eliminate unnecessary references. As Ralph Waldo Emerson once said, "I hate quotations."
8. Who needs rhetorical questions?
9. Exaggeration is a billion times worse than understatement.
10. Last but not least, avoid clichés like the plague.

Ignoring this major flaw in the plan, in 1762, an Oxford professor called Robert Lowth produced a prescriptive text titled *A Short Introduction to English Grammar*, a publication so influential that it dominated grammar teaching into the twentieth century (and indeed is quoted in this book). Over time, one no longer dared to end a sentence with a preposition, to split an infinitive, or to say "between you and I."

> ☛ **Teacher's Corner:** When grammar became a required subject in many U.S. schools in the mid-nineteenth century, teachers complained that they knew no more about it than their pupils.

Grammar lessons began to fall out of favor as the twentieth century progressed. This book aims to fill in some of the gaps that the education system may have left you with, but remember that English is a rich and fluid language and that one person's unbreakable rule is another person's insufferable pedantry. Knowing the rules—and breaking them because you feel like it, not because you don't know any better—will make you a more confident, creative, and entertaining writer and speaker.

If your reaction to that is along the lines of "Yeah, right," consider this: When you're chatting among friends, it may not much matter how you express yourself, but what about when you are applying for a job? Language is as much a part of how you present yourself—and how other people react to you—as the way you dress. if we alwez rote howeva we pleazd itd b like showing up 2 an interview in ript jeanz n a scruffy t-shirt, y'know?

1

Spelling
and Confusables

ABC: Easy as 1, 2, 3 (or, Spelling)

"My spelling is Wobbly. It's good spelling but it
Wobbles, and the letters get in the wrong places."
—A. A. Milne, *Winnie the Pooh*

In the late-1500s, the state of English **spelling** and the "invasion" of foreign words was so troubling to scholars and teachers that some of them took it upon themselves to harness the language by compiling dictionaries. But even if we have the help of education and dictionaries, spelling can still be an uphill climb.

> ✋ **Smart Aleck:** More than one-tenth of English words are not spelled the way they sound.

We have an overwhelming tendency to leave letters in words even though they are no longer pronounced (think of the *g* in *weight* or *daughter*, for example, or the *b* in *subtle*, or the *p* in *pneumonia*). And we are surely the only language to have nine ways to pronounce a single four-letter combination:

A rough-coated, dough-faced, thoughtful ploughman strode through the streets of Scarborough; after falling into a slough, he coughed and hiccoughed.

Then we have things called **eye rhymes,** which are words that look alike and perhaps used to rhyme but which, due to shifts in pronunciation, no longer do. In Shakespeare's day, for example,

> *Blow, blow thou winter wind*
> *Thou art not so unkind*

would probably have rhymed, as would have

> *I am monarch of all I survey...*
> *From the centre all round to the sea*

when poet William Cowper wrote those lines nearly two hundred years later. Then there is another problem. Many words that sound the same are spelled differently:

aloud/allowed	*fair/fare*	*pale/pail*
beach/beech	*knot/not*	*plane/plain*

which makes English a wonderful language for puns but a nightmare for non-native speakers and for those who aren't confident in their spelling (or who rely on their spellcheckers).

"They went and told the sexton, and
The sexton toll'd the bell."
—Thomas Hood

🖐 **Smart Aleck:** A **homophone** is a word that is pronounced the same as another word but differs in meaning. The words may be spelled the same or differently.

It's My Bizness to Be Definate

Here are the correct spellings of a random selection of commonly misspelled words:

accidentally	*cemetery*	*liaison*
accommodate	*definite*	*millennium*
allege	*diarrhea*	*necessary*
avocado	*ecstasy*	*niece*
association	*embarrass*	*privilege*
broccoli	*grammar*	*separate*
business	*height*	*sincerely*

Take My Advice

In these commonly confused noun/verb pairs, the noun has a *c* and the verb has an *s*.

Noun	**Verb**
advice	*advise*
device	*devise*
prophecy	*prophesy*

Useful mnemonic: *I'd advise you not to give advice.*

➤ **Teacher's Corner:** Until the eighteenth century, English spelling was not standardized on either side of the Atlantic. Then, in 1755, Samuel Johnson published his *Dictionary of the English Language*, and in 1828, Noah Webster published *An American Dictionary of the English Language*.

Webster was an orderly minded man who disapproved of a lot of the spelling that Johnson had recorded. (Indeed, he disapproved of a lot about Johnson, saying that he was "naturally indolent and seldom wrote until he was urged by want. Hence…he was compelled to prepare his manuscripts in haste.")

Webster's dislike of words that weren't pronounced the way they looked led him to decree that words such as *centre* and *theatre* should be spelled *center* and *theater;* he also dropped the silent *u* from words such as *colour, favour,* and *honour.* In fact, Webster was singlehandedly responsible for most of the differences between British and American spelling that survive to this day.

Seize the Sieve: A Spelling Rule

The most famous **spelling rule** is *i before e except after c,* although this does not work for *ancient, foreign, neither, protein, science, seize, species, vein* or lots of other words. It really applies only to certain words in which the *ie* or *ei* makes an *ee* sound: *achieve, receive, deceive.*

So even the most famous spelling rule works only in a very limited set of circumstances. There is really no way around this other than reading a lot, taking note of unfamiliar words, and investing in a good dictionary.

One Word or Two?

As a general rule, one word tends to be an adjective, while two words form the noun. Here are some common confusions:

alot/a lot

There is no such word as *alot. A lot* of people know that *a lot* should be two words. If you mean to write the verb *allot,* however, you should allot it two *l*s.

alright/all right

According to *Merriam-Webster's Dictionary*, the term *alright* has had its critics since the early twentieth century. Although *alright* is less frequent than *all right*, it is still commonly used.

> Useful mnemonic: *don't worry about getting it all right, alright?*

altogether/all together

Altogether, *it's sixty miles.*
All together now: "sixty miles to go..."

anyone/any one

*Does this bag belong to **anyone**?*
*It could belong to **any one** of those tourists over there.*

always/all ways

*I **always** get lost in Rome.*
*All **ways** lead to Rome.*

cannot/can not

Either is acceptable, but *cannot* is more common. Sometimes *can not* may be the better choice if you want to be emphatic: *No, you **can not** speak Swahili.*

everyday/every day

*His **everyday** life is very dull, but at night he's in a cabaret act.*
Every day I dream of becoming a showgirl.

everyone/every one

Everyone has a guilty secret.
Every one of you pretends not to like Barry Manilow.

into/in to

> *I can't seem to get **into** the office.*
> *I was hoping to go **in to** use the free Internet.*

maybe/may be

> ***Maybe** you'll remember what I tell you in the future.*
> *Although it **may be** that I forgot to tell you in the first place.*

nobody/no body, somebody/some body, anybody/any body

> ***Nobody** was at the crime scene, so I assumed they'd all gone
> home.*
> *There was a lot of blood at the crime scene, but **no body**.*
> *I think **somebody** is trying to break in.*
> *Gosh, that burglar has quite **some body**.*
> *Will just **any body** suffice for the bikini advertisement, or does
> **anybody** here happen to have Pamela Anderson's address?*

sometimes/some times

> ***Sometimes** trains arrive on time.*
> ***Some times** on that train schedule I gave you are wrong.*
> *I'll give you a call **sometime**.*
> *Perhaps we can arrange **some time** for ourselves.*

I'll Get My Coat

When two words are combined to form a single word, the new
word is called a **portmanteau.** As Humpty Dumpty tells Alice in
Through the Looking-Glass, "There are two meanings packed into
one word." For example:

breakfast and lunch	*brunch*
French and English	*Franglais*
guess and estimate	*guesstimate*
information and commercial	*infomercial*
motor and hotel	*motel*
smoke and fog	*smog*

> ✋ **Smart Aleck:** *Portmanteau* is itself made up of two words, the French *porter* (to carry) and *manteau* (cloak or mantle).

What's the Word I'm Looking for?

abuse/misuse/disabuse
To *abuse* something means "to treat it so badly that you damage it."
To *misuse* something means "to use it wrongly."
To *disabuse* someone of something means "to show them that their thinking is wrong."

acute/chronic
An *acute* illness is one that is sudden and severe but short-lived.
A *chronic* illness persists for a long time.

> Useful mnemonics:
> *acute: children are short, a pain, and not cute for long.*
> *chrOnic = Old (lasting a lOng time).*

affect/effect

Affect is a verb and *effect* is a noun. So you *affect* something by having an *effect* on it. (The exception is if you *effect* a change; that is, cause a change to happen.)

Useful mnemonic: **RAVEN,** that is: **R**emember *Affect-Verb Effect-Noun*.

aggravate/annoy

Aggravate means "to make worse." Therefore, while you can *aggravate* a situation, a problem or a condition, you irritate or *annoy* people.

alternate/alternative

An **alternate** *plan* would be wrong. The verb *alternate* means going back and forth between two things, and thus you have *alternate* letters of the alphabet (a, c, e, g, for example). If you mean "another plan," it should be *alternative.*

among/between

Use *between* for two things; *among* for more than two.
Between *you and me, there's no way we can divide these five loaves and two fishes* **among** *our five thousand guests.*

Useful mnemonics:
*be**Tw**een = **Tw**o*
*a**M**ong = **M**any*

amount/number

Use *amount* for things involving a unified mass—bulk, weight, or sums. In general it is safe to use *amount* to refer to anything that can be measured. *Number* is used to refer to anything that can be counted in individual units.

*That's a large **amount** of sugar for one cup of tea.*
*What is an acceptable **number** of sugars for one cup of tea?*

Useful mnemonic: *use **amount** for things we **cannot count**.*

as if/like

Something looks *like* something else—they physically resemble one another.

*He looks **like** his mother and she looks **like** Margaret Thatcher.*

However:

*It looks **as if** a storm is coming.*
*Teenagers use words **such as** "like" far too often.*
***As with** all homework, students can now research geography topics online.*

"Dream as if you'll live forever;
live as if you'll die today."
—James Dean

---

complement/compliment

*May I **compliment** you on your new hairstyle? The color **complements** your dress beautifully.*

Useful mnemonics:

*A compl**E**ment adds something to make it **E**nough.*
*A comp**LIME**nt puts you in the **LIME**light.*

continual/continuous

Continual means "happening over and over and over again"; *continuous* means "happening constantly without stopping." You

[23]

may *continually* receive unwanted telephone calls from telemarketers. However, if this were happening *continuously*, you would never be able to put the phone down.

Useful mnemonics:

continuAL = Able to Leave off

continuouS = never Stopping

defuse/diffuse

You *defuse* a situation, by (metaphorically) taking the *fuse* out of it before it catches fire.

Diffuse means "to spread out" if it is a verb, or "already spread out" if it is an adjective.

due to/owing to

Due to means "caused by."

Owing to means "because of."

To determine which to use, decide whether you would replace *due to* or *owing to* by *caused by* or *because of.*

> The collapse of hundreds of buildings was **due to** the earthquake.

> **Owing to** collapsed roads and bridges, it was impossible to get outside help.

elude/allude

> Your meaning **eludes** me. I do not understand to what you are **alluding**.

farther/further

This is another example where the difference between words is becoming blurred, but generally speaking *farther* relates to a physical distance, *further* to metaphorical distance.

*Before we travel any **farther**, let's have a **further** look at the map.*

*Before we take this argument any **further**, how much **farther** is it to the hotel?*

Useful mnemonic: ***FAR**ther is about how **FAR**.*

fortuitous/fortunate

Fortuitous means "happening by chance" but not necessarily a *fortunate* chance.

forward/foreword

Useful mnemonics:

*Forw**A**rd means to **A**dvance.*

*Foreword: the **W**OR**D**s that come be**FORE** the main text*

hear/here

Useful mnemonics:

*One h**EAR**s with one's **EAR**s.*

*I want **HER** to come **HER**e.*

hanged/hung

Pictures or jackets are *hung*; criminals used to be *hanged*.

imply/infer

Speakers *imply* something by hinting at it; listeners *infer* something based on the information they hear.

*I **infer** from your tone that you are angry with me.*

*I didn't mean to **imply** that.*

lay/lie/laid

You *lie* in bed but *lay* the book on the table or (if you are a hen) *lay* an egg.

In the past tense, you *lay* in bed all day yesterday, but you *laid* the book or the egg.

So *lie* is the present tense of an intransitive verb that means "to put oneself or to remain in a more or less horizontal position."*
The present participle is *lying,* the past tense is *lay,* and the past participle is *lain.*

Lay is the present tense of a transitive verb whose basic meaning is "to place something in a more or less horizontal position."
The present participle is *laying;* the past tense and the past participle are *laid.*

In the sense of telling an untruth, the forms are *lie, lying,* and *lied.*

lend/loan

Lend is a verb, *loan* is normally a noun.

*If she asks me for a **loan**, I will **lend** her the money.*

Useful mnemonics:

*People will gr**OAN** if you ask them to l**OAN**.*
*People will s**END** if you ask them to l**END**.*

Increasingly *loan* is used as a verb: *the bank will **loan** you the money if you have enough security.* Not everybody likes this, but it's in the dictionaries.

less/fewer

Less means "not as much." *Fewer* means "not as many."
Or, if you prefer, *fewer* is used to denote things that can be counted and *less* to describe things that can't. Never refer to *less people.* People should stand up and be counted!

---

*For more on verbs, see page 68. For more on tenses, see page 76.

loose/lose

Count the *o*s and remember: *if I* **lose** *any more weight, my clothes will be too* **loose**.

older/elder

An *elder* is a person in old age or a tree. As an adjective, it means *older*, but it is sometimes used to denote respect: *an* **elder** *statesman* or even *my* **elder** *sister* may be assumed to have attained a certain amount of wisdom.

Older just means "more old," the way you sometimes feel in the morning, or when you are talking to someone who's never heard of Bob Dylan.

oral/aural/verbal

Oral pertains to the mouth, *aural* to the ears, *verbal* to words. An *oral statement* means one that is not written down. An *oral examination* may be one that is not written down, or it may be performed by a dentist. An *oral/aural examination* may be in a foreign language to test how well you understand what you are hearing as well as how well you speak. A *verbal statement* is a tautology (unnecessary repetition of meaning): how would you make it without using words?

principal/principle

Useful mnemonic: *the principAL is your PAL; she makes ruLEs called principLEs.*

rob/steal

You *rob* a person and *steal* a thing, but not the other way round.

Useful mnemonic: *you can* **rob** *Rob, and you can* **steal** *steel, but you can't* **steal** *Rob and you can't* **rob** *steel.*

stationary/stationery
Stationery is sold at the bookstore. The store is likely to be *stationary*.

their/there/they're
Their means "belonging to them."
There means "in that place."
They're means "they are."

> Useful mnemonic:
> *They left t**HEIR** money to their son and **HEIR**.*
> ***W**HERE shall we place ourselves, **HERE** or t**HERE**?*
> ***THEY'RE** mad at **THEIR** son, who is standing over **THERE**.*

weather/whether
> *I do not know **whether** he is **weather**-wise.*

> "Whether the weather be fine,
> Whether the weather be not,
> We must weather the weather,
> Whatever the weather,
> Whether we like it or not."
> —Unknown

THAT WHICH COMES FIRST (OR, PREFIXES)

A **prefix** is a group of letters added to the beginning of a word to change its meaning. Common ones include:

anti	*extra*	*mono*	*pseudo*
auto	*hyper*	*multi*	*re*
circum	*inter*	*omni*	*sub*
demi	*intra*	*photo*	*tele*
dis	*mega*	*pre*	*trans*

Rule: Adding a prefix does not change the spelling of the original word, nor usually the spelling of the prefix, even when the last letter of the prefix and the first letter of the original word are the same: *disservice, dissimilar, unnerve, unnecessary.*

> ✋ **Smart Aleck:** What of *dispirited*? And *transubstantiation*? **Answer:** There are always exceptions. *Always* being one of them.

All's Well That Starts Well...

Rule: When *all* and *well* are used as prefixes, take away one *l*—*altogether, welfare.* But note that this is not the case with hyphenated words: *all-embracing, well-adjusted, well-bred.*

The prefixes *dis-, il-, im-, in-, ir-, mis-,* or *un-* create words that mean the opposite of the root word (*il-, ir-,* and *im-* are all variants of *in-*, used respectively in front of words beginning with *l*, *r*, and *b*, *m*, or *p*): *disobey, illogical, impossible, inapplicable, irresponsible, misunderstood, unattainable.*

But be careful when a root word can take two or more of these prefixes, since the resulting words will have subtly or completely different meanings: *do I **disremember** or **misremember**? I can't remember.*

> *The loss of paid overtime left most of the workers **dis**affected. The only ones who were **un**affected by this decision were those who never worked overtime.*

> *I collected my children's **dis**used toys, intending to donate them to the fundraiser. However, years of **mis**use had left many of them fit only for the trash.*

> *He was a **dis**interested lawyer and therefore **un**interested in taking a bribe.*

HAPPY ENDINGS
(OR, SUFFIXES)

Suffixes are added to the *end* of a word to change its meaning. Common ones include:

–ant	*–ise*	*–ful*
–ent	*–ist*	*–ness*
–ible	*–fy*	*–ism*
–ing	*–ly*	*–ment*
–ize	*–able*	*–ation*

Adding a suffix may alter the spelling of the preceding word. If a word ends in a *y* that is preceded by a consonant (*happy, beauty*), the *y* changes to *i*:

happy	*happiness*
beauty	*beautiful*

But if the *y* is preceded by a vowel, the *y* remains: *I envy your enjoyment of the situation. It obviously caused you much merriment.* And if the original word ends in an *e*, this is usually dropped: *You are most **lovable** but not at all **sensible**.*

> 🖐 **Smart Aleck:** Hold on to the *e* if dropping it would alter pronunciation. *Pronouncable* would be pronounced *pronounkable*, but *pronounceable* is quite *manageable*.
> Actually, both *aging* and *ageing* are correct.
> As are *likable* and *likeable*.

"-able" and "-ible"

It's not easy to remember which words end in *–able* and which in *–ible*, and there certainly isn't a hard and fast rule. Too much of it depends on the Latin root and whether the word comes to us directly from Latin or via French. Wouldn't you rather just invest in a decent dictionary and look each word up as the necessity arises?

☞ **See Me after Class:**
*She stopped using a curling iron because
she kept singing her hair.*
I don't think I know that tune.

Romeo was dyeing to see Juliet.
Did she insist on a new color?

Toad was carless to wreck his car.
He was afterward!

LIVING LARGE
(OR, CAPITALIZATION)

A **capital letter** is the Large Letter that is used at the beginning of a sentence and as the first letter of certain words. The word comes from the Latin *capitalis,* derived from *caput,* a head.

Use a capital letter...

- for the first word of a sentence

- for the first word in a line of poetry (usually)

- for the major words in the titles of books, plays, films, works of art: *Death of a Salesman, The Catcher in the Rye, Casablanca, The English Patient, Starry Night*

- for proper nouns: *James, Dad (*but *my dad), the Queen*

- for place names and the names of buildings: *London, Paris, Easy Street, the Taj Mahal, the Sears Tower*

- for adjectives derived from proper nouns: *English, Shakespearean, Victorian*

- for the pronoun *I*
- for personal titles that come before a name: *Mr., Ms., Mrs., Dr., Captain, Reverend, Senator*
- for most letters in words that are acronyms: *NASA, NATO*
- for the months of the year, days of the week, and special occasion days: Christmas, Easter, Thanksgiving, Happy Birthday (but *in the new year* or *his birthday seemed to come around faster each year*)
- for brand names: *Kleenex, Mars, Cadillac*

Do Not Use a Capital…

- after a semicolon
- when talking about kings, queens, presidents, and generals in general, rather than a specific individual
- for the seasons—spring, summer, autumn, winter
- for compass points: *north, south, east, west, going north, heading south.* However do write *the South,* as in *the Civil War was fought between the North and the South* or *the South Pole*

> ➤ **Teacher's Corner:** Capital letters are sometimes referred to as "upper case." This is because manual typesetters kept these letters in the upper drawers of a desk—the upper type case. More frequently used letters were stored on a lower shelf, thus "lower case" letters.

TAKE A LETTER
(OR, VOWELS AND CONSONANTS)

"Always end the name of your child with a vowel,
so that when you yell, the name will carry."
—*Bill Cosby*

The word *vowel* derives from the Latin word *vox*, meaning "voice." The dictionary definitions of a **vowel** are a bit scary: "a voiced speech sound whose articulation is characterized by the absence of a friction-causing obstruction in the vocal tract, allowing the breath stream free passage" or "a speech sound made with vibration of the vocal cords but without audible friction, more open than a consonant and capable of forming a syllable." But actually, that "capable of forming a syllable" part is what matters. You can't form a syllable—and therefore can't make a word—without a vowel.

There are five vowels in English: *A, E, I, O,* and *U.*

Useful mnemonic: *An Elephant In Orange Underwear*
But the letter *y,* although classified as a consonant and used as one in words such as *yellow, young,* and *beyond,* is often used as a vowel (with an *i* sound) in words such as *cry, fly, lynx,* and *rhythm.*

Consonants, by the way, are all the letters that aren't vowels.

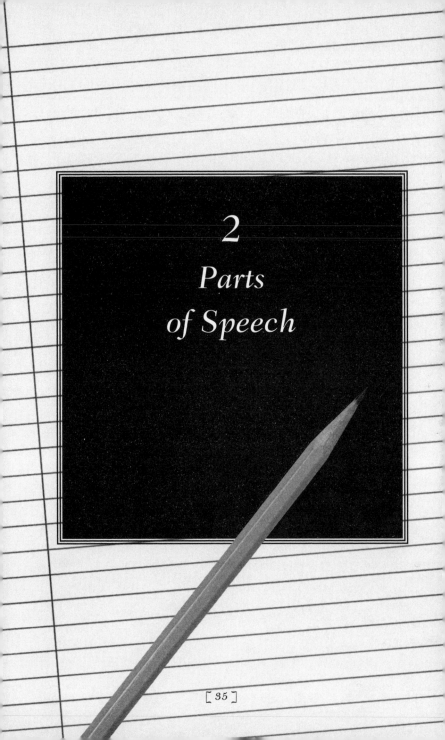

2

Parts
of Speech

SAY WHAT?
(OR, THE 8 PARTS OF SPEECH)

Every word in every language can be categorized according to its grammatical function, which is what we mean by **parts of speech**. As with so many other things, this system was invented by the ancient Greeks, copied by the Romans, and later adopted into English by scholars who were well versed in Latin, whether it was appropriate or not. (In many cases it was not appropriate, but we're stuck with it now, and that's what this book is all about.)

In English there are generally considered to be eight parts of speech: *noun, pronoun, adjective, verb, adverb, preposition, conjunction,* and *interjection,* and you may once have learned this useful piece of doggerel to help you remember what each did:

Every name is called a NOUN,
*As **field** and **fountain**, **street** and **town**;*

In place of noun the PRONOUN stands
*As **he** and **she** can clap **their** hands;*

The ADJECTIVE describes a thing,
*As **magic** wand and **bridal** ring;*

The VERB means action, something done -
*To **read**, to **write**, to **jump**, to **run**;*

How things are done, the ADVERBS tell,
*As **quickly, slowly, badly, well**;*

The PREPOSITION shows relation,
*As **in** the street, or **at** the station;*

CONJUNCTIONS join, in many ways,
*Sentences, words, **or** phrase **and** phrase;*

*The INTERJECTION cries out, "**Hark!***
I need an exclamation mark!"

Through poetry, we learn how each
of these make up THE PARTS OF SPEECH.

We say "generally considered" because there are also three little words—*the, a* and *an*—and a few others that are categorized as **articles** or **determiners** and you can't really ignore them. We'll come back to them in a minute (see page 39), but first let's have a quick look at what parts of speech are all about.

It's Just One Thing After Another

Words from each of the parts of speech are used as **building blocks**: they add to meaning by modifying or qualifying one another. Consider this sentence:

A brown cow in a great, green field ate grass greedily.

By painting a more detailed picture, words limit (modify, qualify—you'll come across all these words to describe the same sort of thing) and thus clarify meaning. In the above sentence, for instance, we are not talking about cows in general; the article *a* tells us we are talking about one specific cow. The cow is not any color; it is brown. The cow is not just standing there; it is eating grass. Where is it eating grass? In a field. Not any old field; but a great, green one. How is it eating? Greedily.

In fact, that sentence doesn't cover all the parts of speech, so let's add another few words:

> *A brown cow in a great, green field ate grass greedily,*
> *and gosh it grew fat!*

The conjunction *and* tells us that we are joining one thought to another. The interjection *gosh* gives us an excuse to write an exclamation mark at the end of the sentence. And *it*, of course, is a pronoun that refers back to the cow.

So let's now look at each of these building blocks in more detail.

DEFINITELY INDEFINITE (OR, ARTICLES)

"A horse, a horse, my kingdom for a horse."
—Shakespeare, *Richard III*

An **article** is any one of a group of things. *I have lost an article of luggage*, for example, means you have lost only one bag of several. In grammar an article is any one of the words *a, an,* and *the.*

A and *an* are known as **indefinite** articles because they describe nouns in general. *The* restricts the meaning of a noun to make it more specific. Or definite. It is therefore known as the **definite article.**

A drunk man	any old drunk man (he could be anyone—we haven't mentioned him yet)
The drunk man	a specific drunk man (someone we are already talking about)
A drunk man was lurching down the street.	This implies the man is a stranger to all.
The drunk man was crawling down the street.	This implies the speaker/writer or listener/reader already knows something about this man—he has already cropped up.

Bizarrely, however, when speaking in very general terms, *the* can be used instead of *a* to make something less specific:

There was a tiger in my garden.	an individual animal
The tiger is an endangered species.	that is, all of them
I bought a ukulele.	one specific instrument
I play the ukulele.	I can pick up any ukulele and strum away happily on it.

> ✍ **Smart Aleck:** *The* is the most common word in the English language.

Absolute Zero

Another way to make a statement more general is to use no article at all. This is sometimes referred to as the **zero article** and it usually applies to plurals or to mass nouns (see page 46).

Children are not good with maps.
Shorts are not suitable office attire.
Cats are thankless creatures.
Grammar is hard to learn.

No Need for Introductions...

Pronouns and proper nouns do not require articles. They stand by themselves.

I am not good at grammar.
Ms. Banks is better at grammar than I am.

A or *an*?

Rule: Nouns or adjectives beginning with a vowel usually take the article *an*, while nouns or adjectives beginning with a consonant take the article *a*.

For example:

an orange, a peach
an octopus, a squid
an ax, a chopper
an island, a continent
an orange peach, a red apple

However, as usual there are exceptions to the rule, because some vowels are sometimes pronounced as if they were consonants, and some *h*s aren't pronounced at all:

a unique event, an unusual event
a horrid man, an honorable gentleman
an hour, an hour and a half
a European, an Eskimo
a eulogy, an epigram

We say *a* unique event because we pronounce the letter *u* in *unique* as a hard *y* sound—*yoonique*. We pronounce the *h* in *horrid*, but not in *honorable*.

Similarly, abbreviations such as *MGM* or *SEC*—pronounced respectively *em gee em* and *ess e see*, sound as if they begin with vowels, and so we say *see an MGM film, it was an SEC regulation*.

☛ **See Me after Class:** There is no *h* at the beginning of the word *aitch*.

An Historical Note

Here's a hypothesis—or rather four separate but vaguely related hypotheses—on words beginning with *h* and an unstressed syllable (or why some people say *an history*, *an hotel*, and *an hypothesis*):

1. Once upon a time all educated English speakers learned French and so pronounced *history*, such as the French word *histoire*, with a silent *h*. Appropriately they gave it the article *an*.

2. Some—less well-educated and therefore non-French-speaking—people spoke badly, were lazy about pronouncing their *aitches*, and so got into the habit of saying *an 'istory*.

3. Educated people disliked dropping aitches, so they began to pronounce them in French words that traditionally used the article *an*: *an history*.

4. People spoke too quickly, running together the words *a* and *history*, so that it became pronounced *anistory*. When they paused for breath and separated things out a bit, they thought the word must be *an history*.

Note the inherent snobbishness of these hypotheses. It crops up a lot in the study of language. But whatever the origins of the practice may be, the rule is: if the *h* is pronounced (as in *history*, *hotel*, and *hypothesis*), the correct article is *a*; if it is not pronounced (as in *honor* and *hour*), use *an*.

> ☛ **Teacher's Corner:** Some of those old grammarians who decreed that *an* should be used before an *h* did so because we aspirated less in those days. Aspiration is the release of air that comes out of our mouths when we speak. If you try talking to a candle flame, you should notice that the flame definitely flickers when you say *hotel* or *history* (aspirated), but much less so when you say *'otel* or *'istory* (unaspirated).

DEMONSTRATE YOUR DETERMINATION (OR, DETERMINERS)

In fact articles are a subdivision of a class of words called **determiners,** which include **possessive adjectives**, **demonstratives,** and **quantifiers**.

Possessive adjectives—*my, his, her, its, our, your, their*—perform the useful task of telling us what belongs to, or is related to, something else.

> *The captain stood firm at the bow of **his** ship as **its** deck was consumed in flames.*
>
> *The bemused sailors redoubled **their** efforts and extinguished the blaze without **his** assistance.*

Used carelessly, however, they can cause confusion:

> *Both the fashion editors liked her new hat.* (Whose hat? If you mean that each fashion editor had a new hat that she liked, try, *each of the fashion editors liked her new hat*, and if you mean there was only one new hat, be specific: *both the fashion editors liked Susanna's new hat.*)
>
> *Mrs. Jones and Mrs. Brown disliked their neighbors.* (Whose neighbors? Did Mrs. Jones and Mrs. Brown cohabit and dislike the same neighbors? Or did each woman dislike her own neighbors? Or possibly her own neighbors and the other woman's neighbors, too?)

Demonstratives are the words *this/that, these/those* (which may also be demonstrative pronouns; see page 65). When used as determiners, they precede the noun in much the same way as *the* or *a* but are used to differentiate between things that are near at hand (*this, these*) and things that are farther away (*that, those*). The nearness or farness may refer to time or space:

> *Do I look fat in **this** dress* (the one I have on)*?*
>
> *Ah, do you remember **that** weekend in Paris* (back in the day)*?*
>
> *I have never seen **these** people before* (though they are standing in front of me now).
>
> *If I had known **those** chocolates* (the ones I ate earlier, so

they are now in the past) *had nuts in them, I would have left them alone.*

Quantifiers are words such as *no, none of, either, neither, any, both, few, little, half,* and so on. Again, some of these words may serve as other parts of speech—*either* or *neither* as conjunctions, for example (see page 100) or *little* as an adjective (see page 84). In this context, however, they go before the noun and tell us the number or quantity of something:

Which of the candidates will I back? **None of the** *above.*

Neither *politician has* **any** *charisma.*

Every one of the *candidates is a crook.*

It would be completely hypocritical of me to vote for **any of** *those people.*

Half the *problems of modern life can be blamed on people like that.*

There is **little** *chance of anyone decent winning.*

WHAT'S IN A NAME? (OR, NOUNS)

There are various categories of **noun**, but they are all "naming words." They just name different types of things.

Common noun: a word used to name a person, animal, place, thing or abstract idea, such as *book, smell, dog, forest, leg, delight, boredom, success* and *failure.* Common nouns can be further subdivided into:

Concrete noun: used to name something you can identify with one or more of the five senses *(book, leg,* for example).

Abstract noun: names something that has no physical existence *(delight, failure,* for example*)*.

Proper noun: used to name a specific person, animal, place, or thing. It is usually written with a capital letter to show its importance, such as *President Obama, the Statue of Liberty, Monday, Christmas, Ibiza, and Rolls-Royce.*

Compound noun: a noun made up of more than one word, usually (but not always) two nouns or a noun and an adjective, to make something with a meaning of its own, such as *apple tree, lion tamer, feel-good factor, tan line, lawsuit, science fiction* (or indeed *science fiction writer*), and *will-o'-the-wisp.*

Wikipedia says that English has a habit of "creating compounds by concatenating words without case markers," which is a wonderfully nonsensical way of saying that we just put words together to make other words or phrases: thus a *science fiction writer* is a *writer* who writes *fiction* based on *science*, but there is nothing in the form of the words to tell us whether they are adjectives or nouns or whatever. And as you can see, these compounds may end up as a single word, two or more separate words or two or more words with one or more hyphens. But let's not get into hyphens just yet.

The Numbers Game

Another way of categorizing nouns is to divide them into **countable** and **mass** (or **non-countable**) nouns.

Countable nouns are (reasonably enough) used to name something that can be counted, such as *one plate, two eggs, three sausages.* It's countable if you can ask **how many** *are there?* or state *there are* **a number of** *men/chairs/staplers*—because you can easily count the specific number of items.

A **mass** or **non-countable noun** refers to something that cannot reasonably be counted and therefore has no plural, such as *air, art, milk, money, stupidity, sand*, and *wisdom*. Quantities of non-countable nouns are described as ***an amount of*** hair/sand/garbage, either because they refer to an unspecified *amount* of stuff or because there are too many individual pieces (of hair or sand, for example) to number. We can't ask *how many?* with non-countable nouns (how many milk, how many traffic); it's simply *how much?*

Twelve Items or Less (Less What?)

A common mistake is the confusion of *less* and *fewer.* Supermarkets almost always get it wrong.

Use *fewer* with countable nouns: *12 items or fewer.*

Use *less* with non-countable nouns: *less traffic than yesterday.*

We're All in It Together

A **collective noun** is one that refers to a group or number of individuals; common examples include *audience, class, family, flock, group, jury, orchestra, parliament, staff,* and *team,* and there are many more.

Strictly speaking, all of these words are singular and take a singular verb. Straightforward enough, you might think. The problem is that a collective noun can refer to a whole group acting as a single entity and also to all the members of that group, acting as individuals. Are you still with me?

Rule: We use a singular verb with a collective noun when we mean the whole group acting as one; we use the plural verb when we are referring to the actions of the individuals within the group.

For example:

The battalion lost all its men in that battle.	All of the men died in the battle.
The battalion lost their lives in that battle.	All of the men died but not necessarily all at once.
The group was waiting in the airport bar.	All members of the group were at the bar.
The group took so long drinking their cocktails that they nearly missed their flight.	But they did not all drink the same cocktail at the same time.
The staff has gone crazy.	All employees are acting strangely.
The staff have locked themselves into their offices.	But they are not all locked in the same office.

Some people call this **formal agreement**—when you say *the staff is*—and **notional agreement**—*the [members of the] team are*.

A related source of confusion lies in the names of sports teams. *The New York Yankees*, for example, is not technically a collective noun. It's a proper noun (hence the capital letters; see page 32), and it should strictly speaking—those words again—be treated as singular. So, bizarrely, should *Manchester United, Toronto Maple Leafs*, and the *Boston Red Sox*. On the other hand, there is no denying that lots of people say *the New York Yankees **are** in the World Series*, and frankly only the most pedantic among us (and Red Sox fans) are likely to be offended.

Adjectives treated as collective nouns—*the rich, the homeless, the lonely*—are always plural and require a plural verb: *the rich are getting richer.*

> ✒ **Teacher's Corner:** To avoid confusion with collective nouns, it is often sensible to reword a sentence. Try *The hotel manager is offering members of the wedding party a discount on their rooms* instead of *The hotel is/are offering the wedding party a discount on its/their rooms.*

I'm the Leader of the Pack/smack/shiver

There are scores of collective nouns to describe parts of the animal (and particularly bird) kingdom. Some of them are genuinely useful (a flock of sheep and a herd of elephants, for example, if sheep and elephants crop up in your conversation to any great extent). Others are obscure or just plain silly, but the following pages provide a small sample of them.

What Do You Call a Group of...?

Ants	*A colony*	Dolphins	*A pod*
Apes	*A shrewdness*	Ducks	*A flock, brace (in flight), raft (on water), team, paddling (on water), badling*
Bats	*A colony*		
Bears	*A sloth, sleuth*		
Bees	*A grist, hive, swarm*	Eagles	*A convocation*
		Elephants	*A herd*
Birds in general	*A flight (in the air); flock (on the ground); volary, brace (generally for gamebirds or waterfowl)*	Fish in general	*A draft, nest, school, shoal*
		Flamingos	*A stand*
		Flies	*A business*
		Frogs	*An army*
Buzzards	*A wake*	Geese	*A flock, gaggle (on the ground), skein (in flight)*
Caterpillars	*An army*		
Cattle	*A drove, herd*		
Clams	*A bed*	Giraffes	*A tower*
Cockroaches	*An intrusion*	Goats	*A tribe, trip*
Cranes	*A sedge*	Grasshoppers	*A cloud*
Crocodiles	*A bask*	Gulls	*A colony*
Crows	*A murder, horde*	Hawks	*A cast, kettle (flying in large numbers), boil (two or more spiraling in flight)*
Deer	*A herd*		

Herring	*An army*	Seals	*A pod, herd*
Hippo-potamuses	*A bloat*	Sharks	*A shiver*
		Sheep	*A drove, flock, herd*
Hornets	*A nest*		
Jellyfish	*A smack*	Snakes, vipers	*A nest*
Kangaroos	*A troop*	Sparrows	*A host*
Lions	*A pride*	Squirrels	*A dray, scurry*
Locusts	*A plague*	Starlings	*A murmuration*
Mules	*A pack, span, barren*	Storks	*A mustering*
		Swallows	*A flight*
Owls	*A parliament*	Swans	*A bevy, wedge (in flight)*
Oysters	*A bed*		
Peacocks	*A muster, an ostentation*	Tigers	*A streak*
		Toads	*A knot*
Penguins	*A colony*	Trout	*A hover*
Pigs	*A drift, drove, litter (young)*	Turkeys	*A rafter, gang*
		Turtles	*A bale, nest*
Porcupines	*A prickle*	Whales	*A pod, gam, herd*
Ravens	*An unkindness*		
Rhinoceroses	*A crash*	Wolves	*A pack*
		Woodpeckers	*A descent*

Is It Common or Proper?

Lots of words have come into English because of the man (with the honorable exception of Mrs. Amelia Bloomer, it was usually a man) who invented or popularized the item concerned. At some stage in the evolution of all these words, they would have been proper nouns, and thus spelled with a capital, but as the word became more commonplace and the association with a person was forgotten, the capital tended to be abandoned, too.

The only one on the list below that merits a capital in the dictionary refers back to an inventor who lived in the twentieth century. We give that capital ten years.

boycott	Captain Charles C. Boycott, Irish land agent ostracized by his neighbors in 1880.
cardigan	The 7th Earl of Cardigan (1797–1868), after whom the garment is named. He was clearly a fashion icon of his day.
dunce	The blessed John Duns Scotus (died 1308), one of the most important theologians and philosophers of the Middle Ages, later accused of unsound reasoning. And presumably made to stand in a corner wearing a pointy hat.
leotard	Jules Léotard, nineteenth-century French acrobat after whom the garment is named.
lynch mob	Captain William Lynch (1742–1820), Virginia justice of the peace at the time of the American Revolution; had a fondness for summarily executing people with whom he disagreed.
maudlin	Mary Magdalene, biblical figure often shown weeping in scripture, to describe the excessively sentimental.

mausoleum	King Mausolos of Caria (died 353 B.C.), whose tomb was one of the Seven Wonders of the Ancient World.
shrapnel	Major-General Henry Shrapnel (1761–1842), English artillery officer, who designed a new type of artillery shell.
silhouette	Etienne de Silhouette (1709–67), unpopular finance minister of Louis XV who imposed harsh economic demands upon the French people. His name became associated with anything done cheaply—particularly the simple form of portraiture that became popular at the time and enabled people to joke that the finance minister was saving money on color paints as well as on everything else.
Zamboni	Frank J. Zamboni (1901–88), ice skating–rink owner who invented an ice resurfacing machine.

ONE DIE, TWO DICE (OR, SINGULAR AND PLURAL)

When a noun means only one thing, it is **singular**. When it is more than one, it is **plural**. The rules on how to change a noun from singular to plural start simply but then tend to head out into left field.

1. Most singular nouns are made plural by adding the letter *s*: *book, bell, candle* = *books, bells, candles*.

2. However, if you add an *s* to such nouns as *church, bus, fox, bush, bench, Jones,* and *waltz,* they become difficult to pronounce. Which is why we add -*es* and create an extra syllable: *churches, buses, Joneses...*

3. If a noun ends in *y* and the letter before the *y* is a vowel, again just add an *s*: *key* = *keys*. However, if a noun ends in *y* and the letter before the *y* is a consonant, the *y* must be changed to an *i* and followed by *es*: *lady* = *ladies, gallery* = *galleries*. But, wait, there's an exception: This rule does not apply to proper nouns: *one penny, several pennies*, but *Mr. and Mrs. Penny* become *the Pennys*.

4. To form the plurals of nouns ending in *ff*, add that *s*: *cliffs, bailiffs*, and so on. However, words ending in a single *f* or in *fe* need to have these letters replaced with a *v*—oh, and then add *es*: *leaf* = *leaves, wife* = *wives*. Got that? Good, because there are exceptions.

Exceptions to Rule 4

Dwarfs and chiefs
Will cause you griefs.
As will proofs, roofs, safes, beliefs.
Hooves and hoofs can either be,
So, too, scarfs and scarves, you see.
To wharfs and wharves, you may refer,
And turfs and turves, as you prefer.

And just when you thought you were getting the hang of it, humans have one *life*, cats have nine *lives*, but artists can paint as many still *lifes* as they like.

5. Many words ending in *o* can be made plural by adding *-s*: *zoos, kangaroos, igloos, solos, sopranos*, *discos, photos, Eskimos, infernos.* Others—seemingly chosen at random—need *-es*: **Buffaloes** *have trampled my* **potatoes** *and* **tomatoes**. *If we sit outside to play* **dominoes,** *we shall be plagued by* **mosquitoes**.

6. A number of nouns have irregular plurals, which is why we do not say *Are you mouses or mans?* and why the plural of *house* is *houses,* but the plural of *louse* is *lice.* Then there's *goose/geese, tooth/teeth, child/children, ox/oxen* (but not *box/boxen*).

> ➤ **Teacher's Corner:** The plural of *talisman* is not *talismen* but *talismans.* Why? Because its origins have nothing to do with *man* or *men.* The word comes to us from Arabic and medieval Greek via French or Spanish.

Rule: The rules always apply, except when they don't. With irregular forms such as *child/children,* sorry, you just have to learn them.

Sorry, Don't Know the Plural…

Dear Sir,
Please send me a mongoose.
Oh, by the way, send me another one, too.

In big-game hunting it appears to be fair game to dispense with the usual plurals. Hence we might shoot *several gazelle, two leopard, three lion, three elephant,* and *six wild pig.* This has a slightly old-fashioned feel and does somehow suggest that you are going out to kill the poor beasts and hang their heads on your wall.

And on the Agendum Today

Some nouns have no (or a rarely used) singular form:

alms	*marginalia*	*tidings*
bellows	*oats*	*tongs*
billiards	*pants*	*trousers*
braces	*pliers*	*tweezers*
clothes	*scissors*	*vespers*
dregs	*shorts*	*victuals*
eaves	*thanks*	*vittles*

Note: Nouns such as these require a **measure word**; for example, *a pair* of trousers, *some* thanks. You cannot say *one scissors*. Nor, happily, can you sow *just the one wild oat.*

"Singularity Is Almost Invariably a Clue"

No, it isn't. That was just Sherlock Holmes being a smart aleck. With some nouns, singularity is more trouble than it's worth.

Such nouns have a plural form but do what the dictionaries describe as "functioning as a singular." Others can function as either a singular or a plural. Which is, frankly, no help at all to those of us who like rules. Still others function as a singular in some senses and as a plural in others.

If the rules don't help, let's try a few examples.

*Mumps **is** nasty, measles **is** measly* is perfectly correct. But so too is *mumps **are** nasty, measles **are** measly.*

Sports with a plural form tend to take a singular verb when we mean them generically, but a plural when we mean something more countable, such as *exercises*. So:

*Athletics **is** tiresome.* meaning the whole concept

*Gymnastics **are** a great way* meaning gymnastic exercises
to start the day.

Pilates, by the way, is the name of the man who invented it, so it is singular. And harder than it looks.

A similar distinction can be made with academic subjects. *Acoustics* is singular when we mean the study of sound, but plural when we mean sound qualities: *the acoustics **were** dreadful.* Similarly, if you study *ethics* or *politics,* it is a singular subject, but if you bring a person's *ethics* into question or complain about company *politics,* they are plural.

One Sheep, Two Sheep...

The following nouns take the same form whether they are singular or plural. What would Sherlock Holmes have to say about that?

aircraft	*kudos*	*shambles*
cannon	*means*	*sheep*
deer	*offspring*	*species*
haddock	*series*	*trout*

Take Your Pick...

All self-respecting pedants know about **Latin plurals**; a smattering (and rapidly diminishing number) of older ones know about Greek, too. But here a little learning can be a dangerous thing, because it is easy to assume that a word ending in *-us* is Latin second declension and therefore has a plural ending in *-i*: *abaci, cacti, incubi, succubi.* Then along comes a word such as *platypus,* whose origins are Greek, and whose plural is strictly speaking *platypuses,* to catch you just when you thought you were being clever. A number of words ending in *-on* are derived from Greek neuter nouns and have a plural form ending in *-a*: *criterion/criteria, phenomenon/phenomena,* and so on.

Some words ending in *-is* are Latin third declension in origin and have a plural form *-es*: *crisis/crises, thesis/theses* (pronounced *-eeze* as in *cheese* or *sneeze*).

And then there are those that have decided to ignore their classical background altogether and allow us to choose between two (or even more) plural forms, some of them rather suspect:

hippopotamus	hippopotamuses, hippopotami
necropolis	necropolises, necropoles, necropoleis, necropoli
octopus	octopi, octopodes, octopuses
oxymoron	oxymorons, oxymora
rhinoceros	rhinoceroses, rhinoceros, rhinoceri, rhinocerotes
syllabus	syllabuses, syllabi
terminus	termini, terminuses
uterus	uteri, uteruses

> ☛ **Teacher's Corner:** *Octopus* is a one-word minefield,
> because it is a Latinized form of the Greek word *oktopous*,
> whose "correct" plural form would be *octopodes*. But
> according to *Merriam-Webster's Dictionary*, today the
> correct form of the plural is *octopuses* or *octopi*.

Keeping Up with the Joneses

When we talk about a family in the plural, we need to add an *s* to
the **family name**; for example, *the Smiths, the Windsors*. However,
if the family name ends in *s, x, ch, sh*, or *z*, we add *-es*: *the Joneses,
the Foxes, the Bushes*.

> ☛ **See Me after Class:** *The Venables's
> came to our house this weekend.*
> Do not make a family name plural by using an apostrophe.

Exceptions: When a name ends in an *s* with a hard *z* sound,
we don't add any ending to form the plural. *We have the Morrises
and the Richards coming to lunch.*

Compounding the Problem

The rule with **plural compound nouns** is to pluralize the base
element of the compound noun—that is, generally, the most
important element of the word or phrase:

> *We have our **mother-in-laws** staying with us, so we stepped
> out for a beer* is wrong.

> **Mothers-in-law** and **daughters-in-law** *don't always get*
> *along* is right.

because the key element of the phrase is *mother* (or *daughter*). Ask yourself *What sort of mother? A mother-in-law.* Similarly:

> *The role of **Secretary of State** varies among countries, and in*
> *some cases there are multiple **Secretaries of State**.*

Doctors Payne and Betterman *were speaking at the conference* (there is more than one doctor, but only one called Payne and only one called Betterman).

> *Bert and Benny were both idle but amiable **men-about-town**.*

The Media Is the Message

In addition to those mentioned above, here are a few more words whose origins we seem to have forgotten, but in these cases— because the plural forms don't end in *s*—we are beginning to use them as singulars. Lots of perfectly literate people now say (and some even write) *The data **was** incorrect* or *The media **is** very hostile to government policy,* but the purists still cling to the distinction between singular and plural.

Plural	Singular
bacteria	*bacterium*
candelabra	*candelabrum*
data	*datum*
dice	*die*
formulae	*formula*
genera	*genus*
graffiti	*graffito*
loci	*locus*
media	*medium*
opera	*opus*
paparazzi	*paparazzo*

One plural that has lost the fight is *pease*, which used to be the regular plural of *pea*. Now *peas* is found pretty much everywhere except in the phrase *pease pudding* and the nursery rhyme about whether it is hot or cold.

👋 **Smart Aleck:** If you add an *s* to the plural words *adventures, bras, cares, cosines, deadlines, millionaires, ogres, princes* and *timelines,* they revert to a singular form: *adventuress, brass, caress, cosiness, deadliness, millionairess, ogress, princess,* and *timeliness.*

By the way, *genie* and *genius* have the same plural: *genii.*

THOU AND THEE (OR, PRONOUNS)

Going back to our poem (see page 37), "In place of noun the pronoun stands," a **pronoun** is used to avoid repeating a noun over and over again. Imagine if you were writing a summary of this book and had to say, *Many people find grammar difficult. Lots of people were never taught grammar at school. Grammar has therefore become a source of anxiety. Indeed, some people might call grammar a minefield.* Just because nobody had thought to invent the words *it* or *them*.

The noun to which a pronoun refers is sometimes called the **antecedent**.

Many people find grammar difficult. Lots of them were never taught it at school.

The antecedent of *them* is people and *grammar* is the antecedent of *it*.

> "The masculine pronouns are he, his, and him,
> But imagine the feminine she, shis, and shim."
> —Anonymous

There are various categories of pronoun, depending on the function they perform in a sentence. The **subject pronouns** are *I, you, he, she, it, we, they*, and the equivalent **object pronouns** are *me, you, him, her, it, us, them*. If we've lost you here, see page 115 for an explanation of subject and object. But it boils down to the difference between *I love him* and *He loves me*, which could be quite significant.

✋ **Smart Aleck:** Since *pronoun* is a noun, why isn't *proverb* a verb?

The Part about Sex

Ahem. The English language does not have a **singular pronoun** that encapsulates both genders. It used to be that "the masculine was deemed to embrace the feminine," but 1960s feminism put a stop to that sort of hanky-panky and has left us with a grammatical problem ever since. Some people meticulously write *he or she, his or hers*, wherever it crops up, but this quickly becomes cumbersome and tedious. Others go for *s/he*, but that still leaves them with the his/her dilemma. Still others go to the opposite extreme and use *she* or *her* throughout (so the feminine is now embracing the masculine, as it were).

Lots of people nowadays fudge this by using *their* as a non-gender-specific singular, as in *the judge* (who may be a man or a woman; we don't know and it would be sexist to assume either) *adjusted their robe.* It isn't pretty, but sometimes being a purist is no oil painting either.

It's All Relative

The **relative pronouns** are *who, what, whom, that, whose,* and *which,* and their role is to introduce subordinate clauses that tell us more about the noun that precedes them. For example:

> *The waiter **who** served you may remember what time you left.*
> *The girl **whose** name was Sue made a lot of money at her garage sale.*
> *He **whom** the gods love dies young.*
> *He was disturbed by the email, **which** he received this morning.*
> *He was disturbed by the email **that** he received this morning.*

Which can also be used to refer back to an entire clause:

> *The sun was shining throughout the rainy season, **which** didn't seem right at all.*

Excellent Reflexes

> "And not in me: I am myself alone."
> —Shakespeare, *Henry VI*

Reflexive pronouns are formed by adding *self* or *selves* to the basic pronoun: *myself, oneself, yourself, himself, herself, itself, ourselves, yourselves, themselves.* They are used when the subject and object of a verb are the same person or thing:

> *I can look after **myself**.*
> *Speak for **yourself**!*
> *We enjoyed **ourselves** immensely.*
> *The kids can never be trusted to behave **themselves** when the babysitter is there.*

They can also be used to avoid ambiguity. Compare these sentences:

> *Tom had done surprisingly well on his exams. The teacher was very pleased with **him*** (that is, pleased with Tom).
> *Tom had done surprisingly well on his exams. The teacher was very pleased with **himself*** (that is, the teacher was pleased with the teacher).

These pronouns can also be used for emphasis, or to mean "alone, unaided": *I can't see what anyone sees in* Big Brother, ***myself**. Or: *Did you really do all of the decorating **yourself**?*

Overuse of reflexive pronouns in this emphatic sense is one of the banes of modern speech. *I think* is just as persuasive as *I myself think* (we're sorry to be dogmatic, but please bear with us this once).

"Every one to rest themselves betake."
—Shakespeare, *The Rape of Lucrece*

Let's Reciprocate

The **reciprocal pronouns** are *each other* and *one another*. *Each other* refers to two people or things; *one another* to more than two.

> *The two candidates who were still in contention congratulated **each other**. The others adjourned to the bar to commiserate with **one another**.*

What's Mine Is Yours

The **possessive pronouns** are *my, mine, your(s), his, her(s), our(s), their(s),* and *its* (and note that they never—repeat never—need an apostrophe: see page 158 for some common confusions). *Mine, yours, his, hers, ours, theirs,* and *its* tend to be used after the noun to which they refer and mean "the thing belonging to or associated with me/you/whoever":

*He had forgotten his gloves again, so I gave him **mine**.*

*Put that book back where you found it: it isn't **yours**.*

*We were madly envious because their house was much nicer than **ours**.*

I Don't Want to Be Specific...

There are a number of useful pronouns that we can use when we don't want to or are unable to specify exactly what we are talking about: *all, another, any, anyone, anything, each, everybody, everyone, everything, few, many, no one, nobody, none, nothing, one, several, some, somebody, someone.* These are called **indefinite pronouns**.

*I think **someone** is in the house.*

*You've eaten most of the chocolates; there are only **a few** left.*

*In space, **no one** can hear you scream.*

By the way, there is no difference in grammatical terms between *no one* and *nobody, someone* and *somebody, anyone* and *anybody.* For once you can just use whichever you like.

Talking about This and That

The **demonstrative pronouns** are *this, that, these,* and *those*— the same words as the demonstrative determiners we met earlier but used in a slightly different way.

*Please take **this** home with you and study it.*	meaning, perhaps, **this** book
*Take **that** to the cleaners, will you?*	**that** jacket
*I want **these** removed at once.*	**these** dirty dishes
***Those** are no good to anybody.*	**those** old clothes

Let's Investigate...

Interrogative pronouns take the place of a noun in a question.

***Who** is that?*	The answer might be: That is Homer Simpson.
***What** is that?*	That is a picture of Homer Simpson.
***Which** is that?*	Which of the many pictures of Homer Simpson in the world are you talking about?
***To whom** should I give the doughnuts?*	It's pretty obvious, really.

Some Common Confusions

their/theirs/there/there's/they're

> *Their* is a possessive pronoun, showing ownership. *It was **their** version of the story that was reported on the news.*

> *Theirs* is also a possessive pronoun indicating that something belongs to more than one person. *That version of the story is **theirs.***

> *There* is an adverb that indicates a place or position. *My new car is over **there**. **There** is a monkey in that tree.*

> *There's* means *there is.* ***There's** that ring you were looking for.*

> *They're* means *they are.* ***They're** a very happy couple even though they fight all the time.*

its/it's

> *Its* is a possessive pronoun. *We thought the cat was lost, but it somehow found **its** way home.*

> *It's* means *it is.* ***It's** not fair.*

whose/who's

> *Whose* is a possessive pronoun. *The boy **whose** pants were flown from the flagpole.*

> *Whose* can also be an interrogative pronoun. ***Whose** pants are those?*

> *Who's* means *who is.* *The boy **who's** being told off for putting them there.*

Who or That?

Rule: Use *who* to refer to people.

Use *that* to refer to animals or inanimate objects.

> *The people **who** matter will be impressed by this.* (*The people* ***that*** *matter* is not incorrect, but is less formal.)
>
> *The tigers **that** come from Siberia have thick fur to protect them against the cold.*
>
> *The house **that** we used to live in has been knocked down to make way for a supermarket.*
>
> *The song **that** he wrote never made it onto the charts.*

In the last two examples, the antecedent is the object of the following clause (we used to live in the house, he wrote the song). In these cases, another option is to omit the relative pronoun altogether:

> *The house we used to live in...*
>
> *The song he wrote...*

And, on the subject of which and that, don't miss the exciting installment on restrictive and non-restrictive clauses later in the book (see page 139).

WHAT A TO-DO (OR, VERBS)

> ✍ **Smart Aleck:** When somebody greets us with *How do you do?* why don't we ever reply, *Do what?*

A **verb** is an "action word": *I **do**, you **go**, he **runs**, we **sleep**, they **sneeze**.* A verb also expresses a state of being: *I **am**, it **is**, we **live**.*

Verbs have a lot of clout. They make things happen.

I books

You grammar

We money

mean nothing without a verb.

*I **write** books*

*You **learn** grammar*

*We **earn** money*

make perfect sense and are good things—particularly the last one.

To Be or Not to Be

With verbs, we start with the **infinitive**, which is made up of the preposition *to* and the basic form of the verb:

***To be**, or not **to be**, that is the question.*

***To sleep**, perchance **to dream**.*

***To have** and **to hold**.*

These verbs have meaning—we know what *to be, to sleep, to dream, to have, to hold* mean—but they don't tell us anything specific about the action that is being performed, the time it is (or was or will be or may have been) being done, or the number of people doing it. For that, we need either:

to **conjugate** the verb—that is, change the ending to show a change of meaning (*he laughs, I laughed*)

or

to add an **auxiliary** or helping verb to specify time and number (*I **will** laugh, you **are** laughing, he **has** laughed*).

Once you have conjugated a verb and added any auxiliaries you want to make the action complete, you have a **finite verb**. (As in, not an infinitive, you see? Clever, right?)

To Boldly Split

The old rule was simple*: never split an infinitive*—that is, on pain of death, never put a word between the *to* and the rest of the verb. The example everyone trundles out at this point is *Star Trek*'s "To boldly go…"

It is, however, probably one of the sillier rules to come out of the old grammarians' insistence on applying Latin rules to English: Latin infinitives are one word—*amare, potare, studere*—so they couldn't be split anyway. Modern scholars believe that splitting an infinitive is perfectly acceptable if the alternative would be clumsy or ambiguous. In the following sentences, for example, we think that the non-split version is more elegant, and the meaning is equally clear, so it is preferable. But it is surely preferable *because it is more elegant*, not because the infinitive is unsplit.

*Many people choose **to incorrectly split** an infinitive in everyday speech.* ☒

*Many people **incorrectly choose to split** an infinitive in everyday speech.* ☑

*They decided **to quickly devour** the pie.* ☒

*They decided **to devour the pie quickly**.* ☑

*She put aside extra time **to closely mark** the exam papers.* ☒

*She put aside extra time **to mark the exam papers closely**.* ☑

On the other hand, this fragment (from the British newspaper the *Daily Telegraph*) scrupulously avoids splitting the infinitive and in so doing sacrifices clarity: *A family doctor who installed a camera **secretly to film** a woman using his bathroom…* What was it that was done secretly? The installation or the filming? (Or, given the context, perhaps both?)

"The English-speaking world may be divided into
(1) those who neither know nor care what a split infinitive
is; (2) those who do not know but care very much;
(3) those who know and condemn; (4) those who know
and approve; (5) those who know and distinguish...
Those who neither know nor care are the vast majority,
and are a happy folk, to be envied by
most of the minority classes."
—H. W. Fowler, *Modern English Usage*, 1926

A Few Irregularities

Regular verbs—those that follow the rules—are conjugated as
follows:

Present tense:	*I love, you love, he loves, we love, they love*
Past tense:	*I loved, you loved, he loved, we loved, they loved*
Present participle:	*loving, biting.*

(Note that if a verb ends in *e*, we drop the *e* to form the present
participle. If not, we just add *-ing*: *wanting, hanging, staggering*,
for example.)

Because this is English, however, there are inevitably lots of
irregular verbs. Some past tenses and past participles are formed
by adding *-t* instead of *-ed* (see below). Then we have *to drink*,
which becomes *I drank, you drank*, and so on, in the past tense,
whereas *to think* becomes *I thought. To speak* becomes *I spoke*, but
to squeak and *to sneak* are regular and become *I squeaked* and *I
sneaked.*

The most thoroughly irregular verbs of all are the common ones *to be* and *to go*: *I **am**, you **are**, he **is**, we **are**, they **are**, I **was**, you **were***. *To go* is OK in the present tense, but *I **went?*** What's that all about?

Again, it's the irritating feature of irregular forms; there's no apparent logic to them, and you just have to learn them.

Back Me Up, Will You?

Auxiliary verbs are used "to indicate the tense, voice, mood, and so on, of another verb where this is not indicated by inflection." Don't you just love dictionaries? It means they are the little words you stick in the front of verbs. There are 23 of them, which can be learned by singing them to the tune of *Jingle Bells*.

> *may, might, must*
> *be, being, been*
> *am, are*
> *is, was, were*
> *do, does, did*
> *should, could, would*
> *have, had, has*
> *will, can*
> *shall*

So they can express simple things such as *I **am** coming*, slightly more complicated ones such as *it **will be** done*, or even more complex ones with up to three auxiliaries attached to one main verb: *He **must have been** feeling unhappy for some time*.

Must and *may*, along with *should and ought*, are also called **modal verbs**: they give information about the mood of the verb (see page 79), expressing such things as obligation (*you **must** be home by midnight, he **ought** to pay before leaving the restaurant*), recommendation (*you **should** call and apologize*) or possibility (***I may** do as you ask, but then again I **may** not*).

May or Might? Can or Could?

Strictly speaking, *may* and *can* operate in the present tense, *might* and *could* in the past or in the conditional (see page 78).

***Can** you lend me 20 dollars?*	Do you have the money?
***Could** you lend me 20 dollars?*	Would you be so very kind as to entrust me with this sum, secure in the knowledge that I will pay it back?

However, this is another distinction that is beginning to be lost in modern-day speech and writing.

Can/could also indicate *capability* or *possibility*, whereas *may/ might* grant us *permission* to do something.

***Can** I drive your Rolls-Royce?*	Well, yes, if your feet can reach the pedals and you understand the concept of a steering wheel.
***May** I drive your Rolls-Royce?*	Over my dead body.

Most people in the English-speaking world seem to have had a schoolteacher who, in response to the question *Can I go to the bathroom?* would raise an eyebrow and say, *I don't know—**can** you?*

> **☞ See Me after Class**
>
> **Could have/could of**
>
> There is no verb *to of. He could've told me* is a short form of
> *He could **have** told me.*
>
> **Try and/try to**
>
> *Try and* is wrong. *Try to* get it right.

About Whom Are We Talking?

For the purposes of grammar, there are only three **persons** (not
people, there are loads of them) in the world:

first person: the speaker (*I, me, we, us*)

second person: the hearer (*you*)

third person: the person or thing spoken of (*he, she, it, they, him,
her, them*)

In modern English, *you* serves as both singular and plural, but
always takes a plural verb—***you are** my lucky star,* ***you were** made
for me,* ***you drive** me crazy*—even when only one person is being
addressed. *Thou* and *thee* were once the singular forms, but they
are now never used except as deliberate archaisms, in church and
in some dialects.

> ✍ **Smart Aleck:** Many languages have both informal and
> formal words for *you*: the French *tu* and *vous* and the
> German *du* and *Sie*, for example. English only has *you*,
> having done away with *thou* centuries ago. But did you
> know that *thou* was in fact the more informal of the two?
> English has preserved the impeccably polite word rather
> than the chummy one. Now why should that be?

The Voice of Reason

And there are two voices: **active** and **passive**.

Rule: With the active voice the subject acts; with the passive voice the subject is acted upon.

Active: *The teacher reprimanded the boy* because *he spilled milk* on his notebook.

Passive: *The boy was reprimanded* because *milk was spilled* on his notebook.

The two sentences say the same thing but with different emphasis. Using the passive voice too often can make writing dull (let's get on with some action!). However, consider:

*If **it were done** when 'tis done then 'twere well **it were done** quickly.*

*Should auld acquaintance **be forgot**, and never **brought to mind**?*

*Yossarian **was moved** very deeply by the absolute simplicity of this clause of Catch-22.*

*The stars **are not wanted** now.*

The passive should not be ruled out altogether. It may be found to have its uses.

"We have not passed that subtle line between childhood and adulthood until we move from the passive voice to the active voice—that is, until we have stopped saying, "It got lost," and say, "I lost it."
—Sydney J. Harris, *On the Contrary*

It's Raining Pronouns

In English we use a little-known thing called the **weather verb** an awful lot.

It is raining.

It is freezing.

It is in the nineties.

What is this nameless, shapeless *it* that is doing all these things? Well, it is known simply as the **dummy subject,** a handy little word that enables us to get to the part we all love: describing the weather. Without it we'd be going around saying, *The sky is raining, the sun is hot,* and so on, which might—perish the thought—make talking about the weather boring.

Getting Tense

> "They said: 'You're Laurie Lee, aren't you? Well just you
> sit there for the present.' I sat there all day but I
> never got it. I ain't going back there again."
> —Laurie Lee, *Cider with Rosie*

Tenses add time to verbs. They put actions into the past, present and future, the may-yet-be or the might-have-been.

*I **do** ballet on Tuesdays.*	I do this habitually, and will continue to do this.
*I **am doing** ballet at the moment.*	I am doing this either right at this moment—so I can't come to the phone—or over a longer but current period of time: perhaps I used to do salsa but have changed.

*I **have done** ballet for years.*	I did ballet in the past and up to and including the present, but I may be getting bored with it now.
*I **have been doing** ballet for years.*	I did ballet in the past and have continued it until the present time and probably will continue in the future. I haven't finished with it yet. Ballet is here for the duration.
*I **did do** ballet once upon a time.*	I did ballet at some indefinite time in the past. It belongs there. I have given it up in the present.
*I **used to do** ballet, but now I do jazz.*	I no longer do ballet.
*I **was doing** ballet on Tuesdays, but now they've changed it to Fridays.*	I was doing ballet on Tuesdays until recently. I may or may not be doing it on Fridays.
*I **would do** ballet if they hadn't changed the class to a Friday.*	If it could be changed to suit me, I would consider doing ballet in the future.
*I **had done** ballet for years, before I switched to jazz.*	I had given up ballet before I took up jazz. There is nothing to suggest whether or not I am still doing jazz.
*I **had been doing** ballet for years before anyone told me I had a crooked spine.*	I was still doing ballet—the action was ongoing—at some time in the past when something else happened.
*I **will do** ballet again one day.*	I intend to/predict that I will do ballet in the future.

*I **will have done** my ballet exam by the time we go on vacation.*	A future action will be completed by or before a specified time in the future.
*I **will be doing** the ballet recital on Saturday.*	It is definitely going to happen at this specific point in the future.

Exactly how many tenses there are in English is arguable. Some grammarians claim that there are only two: the present and the past. (Presumably they let the future take care of itself.) Some say the traditional number is twelve, though others have described as many as thirty and, just to confuse us, some tenses have more than one name. But here are fourteen that should get you through most situations (or ballet positions).

present simple	*I pirouette*
present continuous	*I am pirouetting*
present perfect	*I have pirouetted*
present perfect continuous	*I have been pirouetting*
past simple (also known as **preterite**)	*I did pirouette, I pirouetted*
imperfect	*I used to pirouette*
past continuous	*I was pirouetting*
conditional	*I would pirouette*
pluperfect/past perfect	*I had pirouetted*
past perfect continuous	*I had been pirouetting*
future	*I will pirouette*
future perfect	*I will have pirouetted*
future continuous	*I will be pirouetting*
future perfect continuous	*I will have been pirouetting*

Judging by Your Mood…

Verbs, like the rest of us, act differently depending on which **mood** they are in. There are three moods: **indicative, imperative,** and **subjunctive**.

The **indicative mood** makes a statement or asks a question:

I'm wet, I'm cold, and I'm hungry.

Winter is almost here.

He will come.

Is that the best you can do?

The **imperative mood** gives us a command:

Chill out!

Do as I say!

Don't eat the daisies!

And even the more politely phrased: *Please look after this bear.*

Easy! Unfortunately the **subjunctive mood** is so complicated that it deserves a subheading of its own.

If Only It Were That Easy

The **subjunctive** sounds scarier than it is and has a tendency to fill people with horror. Let's start with a couple of examples:

*I wish it **weren't** going to snow again* (but it is).

*If it **were** to snow* (which it may or may not do, but we
don't know yet), *they would not be able to get home.*

I were or *it were* may sound odd, but they're right when you are using the subjunctive.

Rule: If you know something for a fact, use *was*. If something is contrary to fact, or if you are imagining a future or different situation to the one you are in, use *were*.

> *When I **was** young* (fact: I *was* young once), *I was taught Latin* (it's true, I *was* taught Latin).
>
> *When he **was** young and handsome* (he *was* young and handsome once), *he was also arrogant.*
>
> *I **was** that man* (you *were* indeed).
>
> *When I was poor (I once was indeed poor), I wasn't unhappy.*

> but

> *If I **were** you* (but I'm not), *I should teach myself Latin.*
>
> *If I **were** to teach you Latin* (supposing that I taught you Latin), *would you study hard?*
>
> *If I **were** to be young and handsome again* (but I can't be, alas), *I wouldn't be so arrogant about it.*
>
> *If I **were** that sort of man* (but I'm not), *you might find me there.*
>
> *If I **were** rich* (but I might never be rich), *would I be happier than I am now?*
>
> *I wish I **were** taller (but I am currently stuck at this height).*

A number of **set phrases** in English—*come what may, far be it from me, the powers that be*—use the subjunctive, but the joy of set phrases is that you don't have to think about them.

"If I were reincarnated, I'd want to come back as a
buzzard. Nothing hates him or envies him or wants him
or needs him. He is never bothered or in danger, and he
can eat anything."
—William Faulkner

Sic Transit Gloria...

A **transitive verb** allows the subject to perform an action on an
object (see page 115 for more on subjects and objects):

> *She slapped his face.*   She *slapped* what? His face.
>
> *He pulled the*   He *pulled* what? The cord.
> *communication cord.*

✍ **Smart Aleck:** Transitive verbs with one object only
are called **monotransitive** (*I corrected my teacher*). Verbs
with both a direct object and an indirect object are called
ditransitive (*The teacher threw me an eraser*).

An **intransitive verb** acts by itself:

> *I sleep.*   I cannot *sleep* something.
>
> *I fall.*   I cannot *fall* something.

Famous Intransitives
"Jesus wept."
—*Saint John's Gospel*
✳
"Thus with a kiss I die."
—Shakespeare, *Romeo and Juliet*

Just to confuse things, some verbs can be transitive when used in one sense and intransitive in another. These are known as **ambitransitive verbs**.

Transitive	Intransitive
*He **drank his coffee**.*	*He **drank** like a fish.*
*She **read the menu**.*	*She **read** during dinner.*
*I **gave up cigarettes**.*	*I **give up**.*
*He **kissed her hand**.*	*They **kissed**.*

Tip: To check whether a verb is intransitive, place a period directly after it and see if it makes sense: *He died. You survived.* But *he hit*. (*Hit* what?) *She threw*. (*Threw* what?) A transitive verb needs an object to complete its action.

Verbal Warning

Verbal nouns or **adjectives** are formed from verbs, but they perform the function of nouns or adjectives, and there are three kinds: **participles**, **infinitives,** and **gerunds**. None of these can act on its own as a verb. Instead, each helps a verb to do its job.

Participles

A **participle** is a non-finite form of a verb used with an auxiliary verb to form some compound tenses. It can also be used in **noun, adjectival,** or **adverbial phrases** such as:

***Going to the casino** is a surefire way of losing money.*	**noun phrase**, the subject of the sentence
*The horse **favored by the tipsters** seemed to lose interest at the second fence.*	**adjectival phrase**, describing the horse
*She stormed out, **slamming the door** so hard that the mirror fell off the wall.*	**adverbial phrase**, describing *how* she stormed out

Infinitives

As we saw on page 69, this is the basic form of the verb preceded by *to*, but it is also used in some **compound verb forms** such as:

*I **was going to send** you my address.*

*I **used to go** to a lot of concerts.*

Or following verbs expressing feelings, or to give a reason for an action:

*I **would love to see** her again.*

***Don't forget to wash** your hands.*

*We **built** a fence around the backyard **to keep** the dog under control.*

Gerunds

"What are all these **kissings** worth,
If thou kiss not me?"
—Percy Bysshe Shelley, *Love's Philosophy*

A **gerund** is a noun formed from a verb by adding *-ing*, so it looks exactly like a present participle, but is used in a different way. *When **the going** gets tough, the tough get going.* The first *going* is a gerund: in this sentence, it performs the same function as a noun. To test this statement, try substituting something you know is a noun:

*When **the exams** get tough...*

*When **the meat** gets tough...*

But in the second part of our original sentence, *going* is the present participle of the verb *to go*, linked to the auxiliary verb *get* to make a complete, finite verb.

Here's another example to help you spot the difference:

*I admire the girl **posing** for that photograph.*	**present participle**, referring to the girl who is posing for that photograph
*I admire the girl's **posing** for that photograph.*	**gerund**, referring to the way she is posing, but not necessarily the girl herself

Note the cunning use of the apostrophe here—it carries a wealth of meaning. And guess what? There will be lots more about apostrophes later in the book (see page 168).

KIND OF FUNNY LOOKING (OR, ADJECTIVES)

Most of us were taught the simple rule: an **adjective** is a "describing word." Adjectives modify nouns or pronouns. They tell us what they are like: what they look like, how big they are, and how many of them there are. For example:

*An **ugly** bug*
*A **lovely** girl*
*A **blue** moon*
***Thirty** people*

Adjectives can be derived from proper nouns to describe such things as historical periods (*Elizabethan, Napoleonic*), literary or musical styles (*Shakespearean, Dickensian, Wagnerian*), nationality or geographical location (*French, Parisian*), or other things more loosely associated with people or places (a *Freudian* slip, *Victorian* values, a *Caesarean* section). The suffix *-ian/-ean* means "of or pertaining to (this person/place)"; *-esque* means "in the style of (the person)": so

Dantesque, Kafkaesque, or *Junoesque.* The last of these, intriguingly, is defined as either "of regal beauty" or "large, buxom, and (usually) beautiful," depending on which dictionary you read. Really, if the dictionaries can't agree, what hope is there for the rest of us?

Most of these adjectives are spelled with a capital letter, though *caesarean* has come a long way from Julius Caesar and is now often seen with a lower case *c.* Foods that are named after their place of origin—champagne, parmesan, and the like—are another vague area: strictly speaking they are based on proper nouns, but the more generically they are used, the more it becomes acceptable to drop the capital. It seems bizarre, for example, to insist on using a capital *C* for *New Zealand Cheddar,* on the basis that the cheese is named after a place in Somerset, England.

A Big Bunch of Adjectivals

A group of words can act as an adjective. If they contain a subject and verb, they are known as an **adjectival clause**. If not, they are described as an **adjectival phrase**. (No, we haven't done phrases and clauses yet, but we'll get there—see pages 125 and 129.)

My colleagues, ***who all earn more than I do,*** *never work overtime.*	**adjectival clause,** describing my colleagues
He is the one person in the department ***earning less than I do.***	**adjectival phrase,** describing the person in the department

A Fine Piece of Writing—or Not?

It is easy to go overboard with adjectives (and adverbs, too, see page 88). The author Graham Greene once wrote:

Adjectives are to be avoided unless they are strictly necessary; adverbs too, which is even more important. When I open a book and find that so and so has "answered sharply" or "spoken tenderly," I shut it again: It's the dialogue itself which should express the sharpness or the tenderness without any need to use adverbs to underline them.

Oh dear—what would he have made of this paragraph from *Tess of the D'Urbervilles* by Thomas Hardy?

The young girls formed, indeed, the majority of the band, and their heads of luxuriant hair reflected in the sunshine every tone of gold, and black, and brown. Some had beautiful eyes, others a beautiful nose, others a beautiful mouth and figure; few, if any, had all... A young member of the band turned her head at the exclamation. She was a fine and handsome girl—not handsomer than some others, possibly— but her mobile peony mouth and large innocent eyes added eloquence to color and shape...

Limpet Adjectives (or, Clichés)

Some adjectives are so often attached to certain nouns that they seem permanently stuck together and have become **clichés**. Please do not stick these in your writing:

absolute truth	*new innovation*
close proximity	*original source*
definite decision	*personal friend*
end result	*safe haven*
free gift	*true facts*
local resident	*unexpected surprise*
major breakthrough	*violent explosion*
necessary requisite	*work colleague*

Rule: Verbs and nouns are the bricks of a sentence. They give it structure. Adjectives and adverbs are decorative embellishments. If an adjective or adverb doesn't add anything, don't add it.

☛ **See Me after Class:** *The object is small in size, square in shape, and blue in color.*
Do not waste words on unnecessary description.
The object is small, square, and blue says it all.

REVERENTLY, DISCREETLY, ADVISEDLY, SOBERLY... (OR, ADVERBS)

"When it absolutely, positively has to be there overnight."
—Federal Express slogan (1978–1983)

An **adverb** describes a verb, adjective, or adverb. Adverbs answer questions such as *how, where, when, how much, how often?*

Many but by no means all adverbs in English end in *-ly* (*almost, once, twice, never, well, hard, fast, soon,* and *there* are all adverbs), and many but by no means all the words that end in *-ly* are adverbs (*manly, beastly,* and *holy* are adjectives and *family, butterfly,* and *barfly* are nouns). But it seems that in everyday speech adverbs are steadily disappearing and the adjectival form is being used instead.

The following are all commonly heard but grammatically incorrect:

*He did the task **clever** and I was **real impressed**.*

*He always drives **careful** so he won't get any points on his license.*

*It rained **so heavy** the roof started to leak.*

*She divided them **fair** but the children still weren't happy.*

They should be:

*He did the task clever**ly** and I was real**ly** impressed.*

*He always drives careful**ly**.*

It rained so heavily.
She divided them fairly.

Note that in the first example, *cleverly* is an adverb describing the verb *he did* (How did he do the task? Cleverly), and *really* is an adverb describing the adjective *impressed* (How impressed was I? Really impressed).

Ones That Got Away

> *He doesn't play fair.*
> *I've got it bad.*
> *They're going steady.*
> *Go slow!!*

All of these are acceptable colloquialisms, but you might think twice about using them in formal writing.

And here's an oddity: *She worked extremely hard. Hard* is an adverb qualifying the verb *worked* (How did she work? Hard). And *extremely* is an adverb qualifying the adverb *worked* (How hard did she work? Extremely hard). Despite the fact that *hard* looks like an adjective, we know that it is an adverb because it qualifies the verb. If you invented an adverbial form for it, you would get *she worked hardly*, which just sounds odd, or *she hardly worked*, which means something altogether different. Go figure.

Correctly Placing the Adverb Correctly

Although **word order** is usually important in English (see page 111), the position of the adverb is remarkably flexible. It may go after the verb, *She answered the question hesitantly,* or it may go before the verb: *She **hesitantly** answered the question.* In fact sometimes it can go just about anywhere in a sentence:

Scarily, *she must have been dancing too close to the cliff.*

*She **scarily** must have been dancing too close to the cliff.*

*She must **scarily** have been dancing too close to the cliff.*

*She must have **scarily** been dancing too close to the cliff.*

*She must have been **scarily** dancing too close to the cliff.*

*She must have been dancing **scarily** too close to the cliff.*

*She must have been dancing too close to the cliff, **scarily**.*

Time, Manner, and Place

As with adjectives (see page 84), a group of words can serve as an adverb in an **adverbial clause** or **phrase**:

*I'll go to bed **when this TV show has ended**.*	Answering the question *When will you go to bed?*
*I'll pick you up **just up the road from the movie theater**.*	Answering the question *Where?*
*Some people do this **for fun**.*	Answering the question *Why?*—or perhaps *Why, oh why?*

That's a Bit Intense

Extra adverbs, used for emphasis, are called **intensifiers**: *soon **enough**, **very** nicely, **remarkably** good, **clearly** inadequate.*

But don't overuse adverbs too much: while adverbs can be used to great effect—

*He is **tremendously** tiresome. She is **fantastically** daring.*

*He's **disgustingly** rich.*—

it is easy to fall into the trap of using them tautologically (unnecessary repetition of meaning). One way of assessing whether your adverb adds anything is to consider a sentence with the opposite:

*She screamed **loudly**.*	As opposed to screaming quietly, perhaps?
*He clenched his fists **tightly**.*	How else could he clench his fists?

These are the adverbial equivalents of *close proximity* and *free gift* (see page 171).

Likewise, don't fall into the trap of using words such as *fourthly*. Where possible, just keep it simple:

First, I heard a bang.

Second, I switched on the light.

Third, I grabbed a hairbrush.

There is no need for *Fourthly, I checked my make-up... Ninthly, I went back to bed.*

Rule: If in doubt, leave your adverb out.

DANGLING BY A THREAD (OR, MISPLACED MODIFIERS)

"80 percent of married men cheat in America…"
(The rest cheat in Europe.)

*

"Set against the murky background of gangland London and missing children—buy yours for \$14.99…"
—Radio advertisement for a book

Misplaced modifiers, **dangling modifiers**, **dangling participles**, **misrelated participles**—these are all expressions that grammarians toss into the conversation on purpose to confuse and embarrass the rest of us. So what do they mean? Well, consider a sentence such as:

Walking down Main Street, the new shoe store caught her eye.

We probably all know what is *meant*, but grammatically what this sentence *says* is that the shoe store was walking down the street. The participle is dangling (or misplaced or misrelated) because it seems to relate to the wrong part of the sentence. *As she was walking down Main Street, the new shoe store caught her eye* is correct and unambiguous. As is *Walking down Main Street, she was thrilled to notice the new shoe store.*

Rule 1: The (unexpressed) subject of the participle clause—that is, the person or thing that is *walking down Main Street*—should have the same subject as the (expressed) subject of the main clause: *she*. Careless positioning of all sorts of modifiers can cause amusement, confusion or actions for libel:

Rule 2: The modifying clause or phrase (*walking down Main Street*) should always come as near as possible to the noun or pronoun it modifies. Otherwise you'll create unclear sentences like these:

- John still attends his local church where he was married regularly.

- We will continue to sell goods to people in plastic wrapping.

- She was taken to the hospital having been bitten by a spider in a bathing suit.

- American Catholic theologians will have to wait and see the exact wording of a French document permitting the use of condoms before engaging in theological debate.

- The mother of the accused said that God would judge her son in a news conference on Friday.

- The bride was given away by her father wearing her mother's wedding dress.

- Q: Doctor, how many autopsies have you performed on dead people? A: All my autopsies are performed on dead people.

"I once shot an elephant in my pajamas. How he got into my pajamas I'll never know."
—Groucho Marx

MAY I COMPARE THEE TO A SUMMER'S DAY? (OR, COMPARATIVES)

"Poets and writers who are in love with the superlative all want to do more than they can."
—Friedrich Nietzsche

Comparatives (which may be adjectives or adverbs) compare two things. We say that one thing is *larger, faster, more lovely,* and *more* temperate **than** another thing, or that it runs *more swiftly, more elegantly, less galumphingly* **than** another.

> *The African elephant has **larger** ears **than** the Indian elephant.*
> *In Aesop's fable, the tortoise was **steadier than** the hare.*
> *Shoplifting is **less evil than** murder.*

Comparative adjectives usually employ the suffix *-er* if the original adjective is short enough for it not to become a mouthful. If it doesn't sound right to add *-er* (*beautifuller? temperater?* Don't think so), use the modifier *more: more beautiful, more temperate.* And if we want to say that it is *less* ugly or *less* beautiful—that's how we do it, however short the original adjective is.

Does it sound right? is often a good rule (the proper term is *euphony,* but *does it sound right?* will do just fine). *More big* when we mean *bigger* sounds just as silly as *beautifuller* when we mean *more beautiful.*

Also, there is the question of ambiguity. *The African elephant has **more big ears than** the Indian elephant* sounds as if the elephants have a collection of ears in large and small sizes.

> ☞ **See Me after Class:** Each comparison needs only one
> comparative suffix or word: *more better* is bad,
> *more betterer* is even worser.

For Better, for Worse

So often, it is the really common words that have irregular forms.

> *The movie he took me to see was **good**, but this one is **better**.*
> *The movie he took me to see was **bad**, but this one is **worse**.*

*My father has **many** mansions, but Donald Trump probably
    has **more**.*
*I have **a lot** of trouble with grammar, but some sports
    commentators have **more**.*
See also **superlatives,** below.

Comparing Like with Like

Most comparatives say that something is *more* or *less* something
than the other something, if you see what we mean. But it is also
a comparative to say that something is *the same* (or *not the same*) ***as***
something else:

*He is **as** cunning **as** a fox.*
*This ring is not **as** expensive **as** that one. (I want that one.)*

That's Superlative

*And the **best** and the **worst** of this is
    That neither is **most** to blame,
    If you have forgotten my kisses
    And I have forgotten your name.*
—Algernon Charles Swinburne, *An Interlude*

Superlatives are beyond compare. Nothing can be better or
worse. They are simply the b**EST**.

*The giraffe is the tall**est** living animal.*
*The Concorde was the fast**est** plane.*
*Churchill was the great**est** prime minister.*

Most superlatives end in *-est*, although not *most*. Nor indeed
worst. And, as with comparatives, neither do longer words. Where
a comparative has *more* or *less*, a superlative has *most* or *least*:

Lord of the Rings *is the **most overrated** book of the twentieth century.*

All's Well That Ends Well *is perhaps the **least performed** of Shakespeare's plays.*

Superlatives refer to more than two things: you can't be the *best* of two players; the best you can manage is to be the *better.*

> ⚑ **Teacher's Corner:** The Swinburne verse above may be very pretty, but it's another example of poets being allowed to break the rules:
> *neither is **more** to blame,* please, Algernon!

The Most Worstest Thing You Could Say

As with comparatives, you need only one superlative, so all of these are howlers:

*It is **most nicest**.*

*I think that's the **biggerest**.*

*She is the **most wonderfullest** cook.*

*He is the **bestest** player the Tampa Bay Rays ever signed.*

*He is the **most best** teacher we've ever had.*

AND NOW WE'LL MOVE ON (OR, CONJUNCTIONS)

Conjunctions are joining words; they are used when we want to join two words, phrases, clauses, or sentences together.

*Friend **or** foe*	*Sad **but** true*
*Old **and** wise*	*Rich **though** poor*

There are four kinds of conjunctions: **coordinating**, **subordinating**, **correlative,** and **compound**.

Coordinating conjunctions join sentences (or parts of sentences) of equal importance. They can be remembered by the mnemonic **FANBOYS**:

For
And
Nor
But
Or
Yet
So

I like cats. She likes dogs.

*I like cats **and** she likes dogs.*	I'm doing no more than stating a fact here.
*I like cats **but** she likes dogs.*	…which is perhaps a bit of a shame.
*I like cats **so** she likes dogs.*	She is doing it on purpose, just to be contrary.

When a coordinating conjunction connects two independent clauses, it is often accompanied by a comma: *Should we run through that again, **or** can it wait until tomorrow?* The comma performs no real grammatical function, it simply suggests that you pause for breath. Which is a large part of a comma's job—see page 136.

Subordinating conjunctions link a main clause and a subordinate clause:

*I feel tired **because** I couldn't sleep last night.*
*I feel tired **although** I slept well last night.*
*I hope **that** I have made enough pizza.*
*I wonder **whether** I have bought enough wine.*

> ☛ **Teacher's Corner:** *Asyndeton* is the joining together of two or more complete sentences without the use of a coordinating conjunction—*I came, I saw, I conquered*—whereas *polysyndeton* is the use of multiple conjunctions, usually where they are not strictly necessary: *His hat and book and pen and pencil.*

Correlative conjunctions are used in conjunction with other conjunctions:

> *She owns **not only** an apartment in town **but also** a country house.*
> *She plays **not only** hockey **but also** lacrosse.*
> *Bob will grow up to be **either** sporty **or** clever.*
> *Bob grew up to be **neither** sporty **nor** clever.*
> *Bob's brother is **both** sporty **and** clever.*
> *I like **both** beer **and** lager.*

Rule: In sentences such as these, decide the position of the conjunction by checking on what follows it. They should be the same construction, whether noun, noun phrase, adjective, clause, or whatever. Consider the difference between these sentences:

> *She owns **not only** an apartment in town **but also** a country house.*
> *She **not only** owns an apartment in town, she **also** rents a villa in Tuscany.*
> ***Not only** does she own an apartment in town, but her parents **also** have a country house.*

In each case, the words following *also* balance the words following *not only*. And if you are remotely interested, see the bit about coordination on page 100.

Compound conjunctions is a fancy term for conjunctions made up of several words, often ending with *as* or *that*:

> *I don't mind family Christmases **as long as** I am allowed to come home for New Year's Eve.*
>
> *We can go **as soon as** you decide what to wear.*
>
> *He built a shed at the bottom of the garden **so that** he would have somewhere to keep his ferrets.*

A Word on *While* and *Although*

Although some grammarians argue that using *while* in the same way as *although* is perfectly acceptable, there are times when this can lead to confusion, miscommunication, and other bad things that grammar rules strive to avoid.

While she was writing, her pencil broke.	No problem here: her pencil broke at the same time as she was writing.
While I like tea, I would prefer gin.	Fine, but *although* would work equally well in place of *while*.
While Cyprus is hot, you can ski.	You're unlikely to misunderstand this, but replacing *while* with *although* would remove any possibility of ambiguity.
While Sally plays the triangle, Judy sings.	Aha. Now we have genuine ambiguity. Does Sally accompany Judy's singing, or is Judy's specialty singing and Sally's playing the triangle? If the latter, use *although*.

☞ **See Me after Class:** *While Father was away, Mother seemed to have a lot of fun.* Meaning?

A Bit of Coordination

Some conjunctions have a **coordinating** role between two parts of a sentence, and positioning them correctly can be something of a minefield. Let's start with *both*. *Both* goes directly before the first word of the two to which it refers. So in the sentence *I was **both** unhappy with your work and your time keeping*, the word *both* suggests that there is more than one person involved—which there can't be because there is only *I*.

The correct versions of this sentence are either:

*We were **both** unhappy with your work and your time keeping.*	I and whoever else makes up the *both* were unhappy with two things: your work and your time keeping

or

*I was **both** unhappy with your work and disappointed in your time keeping.*	I experienced two emotions

or

*I was unhappy with **both** your work and your time keeping.*	I was unhappy with two things

The same rule applies in sentences offering a choice of *either/or.*

Not *They had **either** decided to make an offer for the house in the suburbs or the apartment in town;*

nor *They had decided **either** to make an offer for the house in the suburbs **or** the apartment in town;*

but *They had decided to make an offer for **either** the house in the suburbs **or** the apartment in town;*

or *They had decided **either** to make an offer for the house in the suburbs **or** to pay the asking price for the apartment in town.*

IT'S BEHIND YOU! (OR, PREPOSITIONS)

The word *preposition* means "something that is placed before." **Prepositions** are usually placed before nouns or pronouns. It's their job to show where one thing is in position to another; for example, *The cat is **on** the mat, I was **in front of** you.* Expressions such as *in front of, out of* and the like, made up of more than one word, are known (to the in-crowd) as **complex prepositions**.

If you are unsure what a preposition is, you might like to employ the following sentence:

The squirrel ran ———— the tree.

All you have to do is fill in the missing word. Almost any word you choose will be a preposition. For example:

to	*down*	*under*	*near*
by	*up*	*off*	*along*
around	*past*	*in*	*through*
for	*across*	*behind*	*in front of*
through	*over*	*from*	*out of*

Even *at, with,* and *after* would fit—if this particular squirrel is suicidal or we're in some sort of dream sequence. Others, such as *of, between,* and *before,* do not fit at all here, but you get the point.

For non-native speakers prepositions can be tricky. *I get **down** off the bus* tells us exactly what the person is doing, but most native speakers would make do with *I get **off** the bus*. However, even native speakers often think that two prepositions are better than one:

> *I get **off of** the bus.* ☒   What's that *of* doing there?
>
> *Put that **back down** on the table.* ☒
>
> *I took a day **off from** work.* ☒

Sometimes even one is too many:

> *Where did he go **to**?*
> *She admitted **to** her mistakes.*
> *All **of** the people present at the rally protested peacefully.*
> *I'm going **down** south.*

> ✋ **Smart Aleck:** The use of more words than are necessary is *pleonasm* or *prolixity*.

Let's Not Ask for the Moon

Many prepositions are firmly wedded to other words:

> *I **approve of** his choice. They're **discriminating against** us.*

However, others are more loosely connected:

*When I want your opinion I'll **ask for** it*	…but I might **ask after** your health.
*They've **taken in** everything you said to them*	…but she's **taken off** everything except her feather boa.
*You are **good at** what you do*	…which is better than being **good for** nothing.

Some prepositions tend to ruffle our feathers a bit:

absorbed in/by

*I was **absorbed in** my book.*

*All of a sudden I was **absorbed by** a giant sponge.*

agree with/approve of

*I **agree with** your ideas.*

*But I don't **approve of** children being taught grammar.*

aim at/to/for

***Aim at** that target.*

***Aim to** arrive at work before lunchtime.*

***Aim for** Paris and try to fly in a straight line.*

among/between

*I put the cat **among** the (many) pigeons with my thoughtless comment.*

*I placed a pigeon **between** my two cats to see what would happen.*

bored of

Wrong. We should be bored by or bored with something or somebody.

center around/on

How can something center around something else? Presumably it would need to center around another center. Something centers on something—or is based on it.

compare with/to

*You can't **compare** my feet **to** an elephant's: they are too dissimilar to be compared.*

***Compared with** an elephant's, my feet look dainty.*

different to/from

Many books claim that *different from* is preferable to *different to* without explaining why. However, Fowler's *Modern English Usage* says "that *different* can only be followed by *from* & not by *to* is a SUPERSTITION. Not only is *to* 'found in writers of all ages' (OED); the principle on which it is rejected (You do not say differ to; therefore you cannot say different to) involves a hasty & ill-defined generalization." All of which is a long-winded way of saying that you can say *different to* if you like.

made of/made from

This one is a bit persnickety, but something is made *from* something that has been transformed; it is made *of* something that is still visible or recognizable:

*This ice cream is **made from** raspberries.*	So if you don't like raspberries, have the chocolate mousse instead.
*This pavlova is **made of** raspberries, cream, and meringue.*	So if you don't like raspberries, you can pick them out, and I'll eat them.

✋ Smart Aleck:

Why does your house burn up as it burns down?
How come you have to fill in a form to fill out a form?
Why can you see stars out but not lights out?

Get Us Out from under This

Rule: It is wrong to end a sentence with a preposition. This seems to be a rule for a rule's sake. In fact, ending a sentence with a preposition rarely hinders its meaning and often sounds more natural, certainly in speech. Compare:

That's the office in which I work.	*That's the office I work in.*
The choir shown on Songs of Praise *is the one with which I sing.*	*The choir shown on* Songs of Praise *is the one I sing with.*
About what the heck are you talking?	*What the heck are you talking about?*

Ha-Ha

Suffering from impotence, a man visits several doctors asking for help, all to no avail. Finally, out of desperation, he visits an herbalist. The herbalist gives him a potion that can only be used once a year and tells him to take it before he is ready to be intimate. Then, when the time is right, he should say "one, two, three" and his impotence will be cured for as long as he likes. The man asks, "How do I make the potion stop working?" "Oh, that's easy," the doctor replies, "You just say, 'one, two, three, four.'" That evening before he enters the house, the man drinks the potion. He surprises his wife by immediately leading her to the bedroom. Things are going well and the man whispers, "One, two, three." His wife gives him a funny look and asks, "What'd you say 'one, two, three' for?" And **that** is why you never end a sentence with a preposition!

HOLY MOLY!
(OR, INTERJECTIONS)

An **interjection**—often followed by an exclamation mark—is used to show emotion. It is not grammatically linked to other parts of a sentence.

Bah! Darn! Eek! Good Lord! God bless you! Heavens! Yikes!
Hey! Ouch! Oh no! No way! Nonsense! D'oh!

Well, that was easy, wasn't it? We're not even going to bother to say, "Don't overdo exclamation marks!" at this stage, because there'll be plenty of that when we get to punctuation (see page 145).

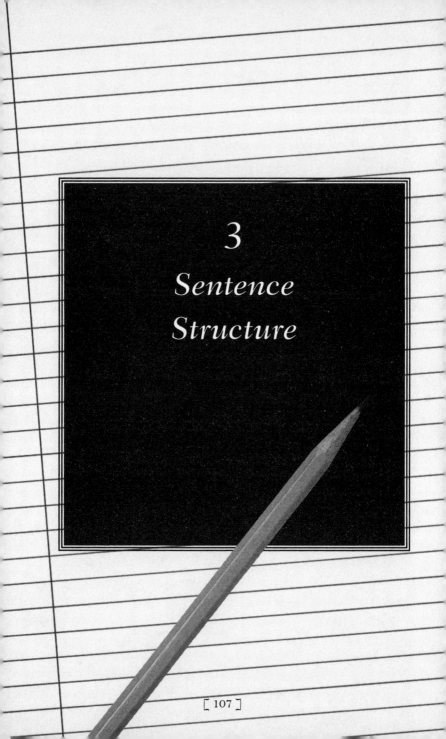

3

Sentence Structure

DO I GET TIME OFF FOR GOOD BEHAVIOR? (OR, SENTENCES)

"A perfectly healthy sentence, it is true, is extremely rare.
For the most part we miss the hue and fragrance
of the thought; as if we could be satisfied
with the dews of the morning without their colors,
or the heavens without their azure."
—Henry David Thoreau

According to the dictionary, a **sentence** is "a sequence of words capable of standing alone to make an assertion, ask a question or give a command." All sentences…

1. Have a subject and a predicate (see page 111)
2. Begin with a capital letter
3. End in a period, a question mark, or an exclamation mark

There are various types of sentences, depending on how complicated they are:

A **simple sentence** consists of a single main clause or statement (we'll come back to what a clause is shortly—see page 125): *I like pink roses*, or *You prefer white roses.*

A **compound sentence** consists of two or more main clauses: *I like pink roses best, but I expect you'll choose white ones.*

Complex sentences have main clauses and subordinate clauses:

The roses, when they finally arrived, were yellow.

Really complex sentences (or **compound-complex sentences**, if we're going to be technical) have clauses coming out of their ears and often get a bit carried away with themselves: *The roses, which you say you ordered several days ago, didn't arrive until this morning, and were yellow, not pink or white by the way, so the bride is not happy.*

> ✍ **Smart Aleck:** The longest sentence in English literature is spoken by Molly Bloom in James Joyce's *Ulysses*. It contains 4,391 words, which makes it far too long to be quoted here.

Fragments

Complete sentences need a subject and a verb. Without these, they are known as **fragments**.

That wretched dress.

Waiting in the mall for her prescription.

Never in agreement about anything.

Fragments need the context of other sentences in order to convey their meaning:

I had an awful time at the party. Sally again. Going on and on about having worn the same dress as that new actress. That wretched dress.

I saw Sally again this morning. Waiting in the mall for her prescription. At least, that's what she was pretending to do. I'm sure she was really watching to see if I bought anything for the weekend.

What Kind of a Sentence Is That?

Many sentences simply make statements. The formal term for this is a declarative sentence. But sentences can also ask questions, give instructions or make exclamations:

A **declarative sentence:** *I saw you copying the files.*

An **interrogative sentence:** *Did you copy the files?*

An **imperative sentence:** *Don't even think of copying the files.*

An **exclamatory sentence:** *I repeat, I did not copy the files!*

Note, by the way, that an imperative sentence doesn't need a subject. In this instance the pronoun *you* is clearly implied.

Imperatives don't have to be bossy, just gently persuasive—which is probably why advertisers love them:

> *Just do it.*
> *Let your fingers do the walking.*
> ***Don't** leave home without it.*

SUBJECT-VERB-OBJECT

Here's a simple sentence: *I wrote a simple sentence.* It is made up of a subject, a verb, and an object. We know about verbs, so we can probably tell that in the above sentence the verb is *wrote*. The rest of the sentence consists of a subject and an object…

Rule 1: The **subject** is the person or thing carrying out the action in a sentence. (In this case *I*. Who wrote the simple sentence? I did.) The **object** is on the receiving end of the action. It is the thing being done to. (In this case, *a simple sentence.* What did I write? A simple sentence.) To determine the subject of a sentence, first find the **verb** and then ask *who?* or *what?* is doing the action. The answer will be the subject.

Rule 2: In a straightforward English sentence the subject will come first, the verb second, and the object third. (Grammarians refer to this as SVO.)

Subject	**Verb**	**Object**
Simple Simon	*met*	*a pieman*
Mary	*had*	*a little lamb*
Little Bo Peep	*has lost*	*her sheep*

Another useful piece of terminology here is the **predicate**. This is the verb and the object (or indirect object, or anything else that isn't the subject) considered together. So, in the above examples, *met a pieman*, *had a little lamb* and *has lost her sheep* are all predicates. So are *sat on a wall*, *jumped over the moon*, *sat on a tuffet* and *went up the hill to fetch a pail of water*. Who would have thought that nursery rhymes could prove so useful?

"Proper words in proper places
make the true definition of a style."
—Jonathan Swift, *Letter to a Young Clergyman*

*

"I have the words already. What I am seeking is the
perfect order of words in the sentence.
You can see for yourself how many different ways
they might be arranged."
—James Joyce

Breaking the Subject-Verb-Object (SVO) Rule

The SVO rule can be broken for emphasis or stylistic effect:

John I can convince	...but James would never let me get away with such nonsense.
Chicken I can live without	...though I am rather partial to duck.

It's also broken with questions, when the verb commonly precedes the subject: *Who was that lady I saw you with last night?*

Direct and Indirect Objects

So far, so good. In some sentences, however, there is more than one object—a direct one and an indirect one.

Take this sentence: *My boss paid me a bonus.*

If you have been paying attention so far, you know that *my boss* is the subject of the verb *paid*. But now you have to ask:

What did the boss pay?	*He paid a **bonus***	**direct object**
To **whom** did he pay it?	*To **me***	**indirect object**

Hang on, you may say, how about *The boss paid me?* Doesn't that make *me* the direct object? Well, no. The test here is to see if you can rework the sentence to put a preposition in front of the object. If you can, it's an indirect object. You could easily rephrase the above example to become *My boss paid a bonus to me.* Clumsy, perhaps, but it makes sense (and it would be absolutely fine if you wanted to say *My boss paid a bonus to everyone in my department*).

Don't trip up on a sentence that begins with *there* and a form of the verb *to be. There* is not the subject in this case: *there were lots of people out for a walk today.* To find the correct subject, ask *who?* or *what?* before the verb. *Who was out for a walk today?* Answer: *lots of people.*

The Exception: It Would Be, Wouldn't It?

The exception to the subject-verb-object rule concerns— guess what—the verb *to be.* It doesn't take an object, it takes a **complement**. *To be,* and verbs used in a similar way, such as *to become, to seem, to taste* are called **copulative verbs** (honestly, they are—look it up in the dictionary yourself if you don't believe us)—they express a state rather than performing an action. So in sentences such as:

> *I am a New Yorker*
> *You became an artist*
> *He seems respectable enough*
> *The chocolates tasted of arsenic*

the words after the verb are the complement, and they may be nouns, pronouns, adjectives or adverbs, or phrases serving the same purpose (in the above example, *of arsenic* is an adverbial phrase qualifying the verb *tasted*).

ON THE SUBJECT OF I AND THE OBJECT OF ME (OR, SUBJECT AND OBJECT)

Unlike Latin, English nouns don't bother much with cases (different endings to show their relationship with other words in the sentence) because we express that sort of thing with prepositions (see page 101) and word order. In Latin a noun would have a different ending depending on whether it was the **subject** or the **object** of the verb, and if you wanted to say *to the noun* or *of the noun*, the endings would be different again. Then you could put the words in pretty much any order you liked and the endings would sort the meaning out for you. But English sentences such as *the dog chased the cat* and *the cat chased the dog* have exactly the same words in them and it is the order that establishes the meaning.

Pronouns don't follow this no-change rule. They do their own thing. Or their own thing is done to them.

Rule: **I = subject**

me = object

I is used for the subject of a sentence—the person doing the action.

Me is used for the object of the sentence—the person the verb is acting upon.

Not *Me telephoned Jim*   Because I performed the
but *I telephoned Jim.*   action.

Not *Jim rang I back*   Because Jim performed the
but *Jim rang me back.*   action.

Similarly: he/she/it/they = subject
him/her/it/them = object

Not *I adore he* but *I adore him.*	He is the *object* of my affection.
Not *Them were responsible* but *They were responsible.*	They *subjected* us to the horror.

This rule applies, but may be less obvious, when you have a **compound subject** or a **compound object**—that is, a subject or object that consists of more than one noun or pronoun.

*John and **I*** (compound subject) *went fishing.*

He gave the bait to John (or ***him***) *and **me*** (compound object).

*My husband and **I*** (compound subject) *are both going to the wedding.*

The groom has invited my husband (or ***him***) *and **me*** (compound object) *to the wedding.*

Hint: If you are unsure whether to use *I* or *me*, or *he* or *him*, in a compound subject or object, take out the other part. If you omit your husband from the last two examples you are left with:

I am going to the wedding (OK, you've had to change the verb from *are* to *am* because there's only one person involved now, but that's not the point here).

The groom has invited me to the wedding.

What's Wrong with Songwriters?

Beach Boys: *"My buddies and me are gettin' real well known..."*

The Beatles: *"Take a good look, you're bound to see that you and me were meant to be for each other..."*

Rule: The rules don't apply to songwriters. But surely they can't get no satisfaction from their writing.

Who Goes There? I or Me?

*It is **I** or It is **me**?*

*It wasn't **I** who said it or It wasn't **me** who said it?*

*It is **I** who am at fault or It is **me** who is at fault?*

> "'Somebody's sharp.' 'Who is?' asked the gentleman,
> laughing. I looked up quickly, being curious to know.
> 'Only Brooks of Sheffield,' said Mr. Murdstone.
> I was relieved to find that it was only Brooks of Sheffield;
> for, at first, I really thought it was I."
> —Charles Dickens, *David Copperfield*

Traditionally, *It is I* is correct, because Latin rules state that subject forms are found after the verb *to be*. However, modern thinking is that this sounds rather pretentious and old-fashioned. Most people will not bat an eyelid if you say *It was me*.

If that isn't good enough for you, try avoiding the issue by rephrasing:

He can't run as fast as me (or *I*) becomes

*He can't run as fast as I **can**.*

He's earning more than her (or *she*) becomes

*He's earning more than she **is**.*

Or, if you aren't happy with that, just decide which way you are going to go and stick to it. This sentence—heard on a radio news bulletin recently—fails on every count: *It was he who fired the gun and it was him who was killed.*

"Heedless of grammar, they all cried, 'That's him!'"
—Rev. R. H. Barham, *A Lay of Saint Gengulphus*

Between You and I

Here's the **I-me error** creeping in again. Lots of people are anxious about using *me*. But—between you and me—it is wrong to say *between you and I*.

Rule: Always use an object pronoun (*me*) after a preposition (*between*). (See page 101 for a list of prepositions.)

They can't take that away from me…

I've been to paradise but I've never been to me…

It's good night from me, and it's good night from him.

"Between you and me and the grand piano, I'm afraid my
father was rather a bad hat."
—*The Uninvited* (film), 1944

My Grammar and I (or should that be "me"?)

Few of us will have cause to ask (or answer, or give a darn about)
this question in real life. However, this book does ask it, so it seems
only courteous to try to answer it:

> *This book is **about** (preposition) my grammar and **me** (object*
> *pronoun).*
>
> ***My grammar** (subject) and **I** (subject pronoun) are not on good*
> *terms.*

In a book title, we think it is safe to assume that *Grammar and I*
form a compound subject (see page 116).

Remember Your Manners

If you are talking about yourself and another person, it is polite to
mention the other person first.

> *Wishing you both great happiness from me and Gary.* ☒
> *Wishing you both great happiness from Gary and me.* ☑
>
> *I and my wife would like to thank everyone for coming.* ☒
> *My wife and I would like to thank everyone for coming.* ☑

But there's no need to be too humble:

> *With lots of love from the children, the dog and me...*

Nor too full of oneself:

> *James and **myself** went fishing.*
> *James and **I** went fishing* will do very well.

On the Subject of Who and the Object of Whom

"What is fame? The advantage of being known by
people of whom you yourself know nothing,
and for whom you care as little."
—Lord Byron

*

"As far as I'm concerned,
whom is a word that was invented
to make everyone sound like a butler."
—Calvin Trillin

Rule 1: **who = subject**
whom = object

*This is the woman **who** swallowed a fly.*	The woman swallowed the fly. The woman is the subject of the verb.
*This is the woman **whom** the fly choked.*	The fly choked the woman. She is now the object of the verb.

Rule 2: As with other pronouns, the object form is used after a preposition (see page 101):

*The people **to whom** I spoke didn't seem to know anything about it.*

*That boy **above whom** we all towered when we were at school is taller than any of us now.*

*Send not to ask **for whom** the bell tolls.*

Don't you Agree?
(or, Agreement)

Rule: Parts of a sentence must agree with each other. A singular subject takes a singular verb, while a plural subject takes a plural verb.

*I **was born** in a caravan.*

***She is** only a bird in a gilded cage.*

*What **were we** talking about?*

***They don't** make them like that any more.*

Straightforward enough? Less obvious, perhaps, are:

*He is one of those **men who sing** in the shower.*	*Those men*, plural, are the subject of the verb *sing*.
*A **person knows** when he/she is being rude.*	Many people nowadays would say, *A person **knows** when they are being rude.* Perhaps better to avoid the issue by saying, *People **know** when **they are** being rude* instead.

And what about:

*My brother **and** his girlfriend (two people) **have** taken the spare room.*

*It sounds as if my brother **or** his girlfriend (one or the other but not both) **has** used all the hot water.*

Rule: Use a plural verb with two or more subjects when they are connected by *and*. Two singular subjects connected by *or* or *nor* take the singular form of the verb.

And another rule: *Either* and *neither* are both singular. ***Neither of them has*** *thought about my needing to wash.* ***Either he*** *or* ***she is*** *bathing last tomorrow, if I have any say in the matter.*

Along Came a Distraction

Sometimes an expression may creep between a subject and its verb. Don't let this lead you astray.

> ***The nanny***, *along with the cook and the housekeeper,* ***has** caught chicken pox from the children.*

> ***Poisoning***, *as well as the shock of the bite,* ***was** the cause of death.*

> ***My husband***, *with our neighbor and his dog,* ***is** walking the coastal path.*

We'll have a closer look at those parenthetical commas in the next chapter, but for the moment just note that they are precisely that—a parenthesis or bracket—and everything between them could be lifted out of the sentence without altering the grammatical relationship between the subject and the verb.

☞ **See Me after Class:**
Each *of the boys* ***were** good at grammar.*
Were he indeed?
Every *cat* ***have their** own bowl.*
No: ***every** cat* ***has its** own bowl.*
Just as ***every** cat* ***has** a tail.*

Useful mnemonic: think of these words as *each one* and *every one*, and you'll remember to use a singular verb and a singular pronoun.

Rule: The following words are singular and require singular verbs:

anybody	*every*	*one*
anyone	*everybody*	*somebody*
each	*everyone*	*someone*

However, *any, all, most,* and *some* can be either singular or plural. It depends whether they are being applied to countable or non-countable nouns (see page 47).

*All of the petty cash **has** been stolen.*

*All of the suspects **have** gone to the pub together.*

*Some of their discarded kebabs **have** been discovered.*

*Some of the money **has** been found.*

*Most of it **is** still missing.*

*Most of the culprits **are** nursing hangovers.*

Rule: *Many, both, a few,* and *several* are always followed by a plural verb.

I've Got Your Number

Numerical expressions can be rather tricky, but just remember that the expression *the number* is singular, which means it should be followed by a singular verb:

*The number **is** 6.*

*The number in question **is** 666.*

*The number of people unaccounted for **is** 6,000.*

*The number of people who died **was** 60,000.*

Exception: *A number of* is used with plural nouns and takes a plural verb:

*A number of people **were** in shock after the incident.*

Numerical expressions, however, take either the singular or plural form of the verb, according to whether they are being referred to as a single entity or as individuals within a group.

*A million dollars **is** a lot of money.*

*A million homes **are** reported to be without power today.*

***Two** years **is** a long time to wait.*

*The **two** years since I saw you **have** dragged by.*

***Half** the people at the party **have** food poisoning.*

*The **remainder** of the guests **are** still enjoying the party.*

And Then There Was None...

You're likely to come across conflicting views on this one. Many people believe that *none* is a contraction of *not one*, and therefore should always take the singular verb. *None* may also mean *not any*, however, in which case it takes a plural verb.

Rule: *None* is singular only when it means *no amount*. If you mean *not one* you could always say *not one*, particularly if you want to add emphasis.

***None** of the wine **was** left in the bottle.*

***None** of the drinks **are** paid for.*

***None** of the food **is** fresh.*

***None** of the people **are** well.*

How Many Objects Exactly?

Another common area of confusion between singular and plural comes in sentences such as:

Many men cheat on their wife/wives?

The boys put their hands on their head/s?

Are we talking about bigamists as well as adulterers here? Or a number of men sharing a single wife? Many-headed boys? Or boys sharing a single head?

Rule: The two elements should agree. ***Men***, plural, even monogamous ones, *have **wives***, plural. ***Boys***, even non-freaky ones, *have **heads***.

Or you can write the sentences differently and duck the issue:

Many a man cheats on his wife.

Each boy put his hands on his head.

FROM MAJOR TO MINOR (OR, CLAUSES)

A **clause** is a sentencelike construction with a subject and predicate, including a finite verb (see pages 72 and 123 for an explanation of those things). Some clauses, but by no means all, stand alone as sentences. A clause that can stand alone as a sentence is known as the **main clause**; anything else is a **subordinate clause**.

I can't play the piano as well as my sister, even though I practice more than she does.

I can't play the piano as well as my sister is a perfectly good sentence on its own. It has a subject (*I*) and a finite verb (*play*) and makes a complete statement. *Even though I practice more than she does* is not. It has a subject (*I*) and a finite verb (*practice*), but it depends on the first clause (*I can't play the piano as well as my sister*) to become a complete statement.

But it's perfectly possible for a sentence to have two main clauses, in which case they are called **coordinating clauses** and are usually linked by *and, but,* or *or*:

*I'm going to play the piece by Mozart, **and** she will play the piece by Chopin.*

*I wanted to play the Chopin, **but** she had first choice.|*
*I might play in the concert, **or** I might decide to go to a bar instead.*

In all these examples either of the two clauses can stand alone.

As its name suggests, a **subordinate clause** carries information that is of secondary importance to that contained in the main clause.

A subordinate clause often begins with a subordinate conjunction such as *after, although, as, because, though, if, in order to, rather than, since, so that, unless,* and so on.

*Unfortunately I won't be playing, **because I've broken my finger.***
*She won the role, **although nobody thought she had a chance.***

Or it may begin a relative pronoun (*that, which, whichever, who, whoever, whom, whose, whosoever, whomever*), in which case it is called a **relative clause**.

*I used to know the spy **who came in from the cold.***
*I used to know the spy **whom the Russians codenamed Smirnoff.***
*I will claim to have known **whichever of the spies you bring into the conversation.***

Which Is That?

Restrictive clauses (also sometimes called **defining clauses**) define or classify a noun or pronoun in the main clause. **Non-restrictive** or **non-defining clauses** offer further description. A non-restrictive clause is usually preceded by a pause in speech or a comma in writing, whereas a restrictive clause is not. A non-restrictive clause is also usually *followed* by a pause or a comma, if it does not end the sentence.

Rule: Non-restrictive clauses are dispensable. Their role is merely to give additional information.

Sorry, have we lost you? Let's look at some examples. Although the following sentences make grammatical sense without their subordinate clauses, they do not convey much information—the restrictive clause is essential.

*The man **that died on the trip** was once my history teacher.*
*The car **that broke down** is now in the garage.*
*You look like the cat **that got the canary**.*

Take out that clause and you are left with:

The man was once my history teacher.	Which man? Why are you telling me this? Why should I care?
The car is now in the garage.	Again, which car? So what?
You look like the cat.	Duh? I think you'll find I don't have whiskers or a tail.

On the other hand,

*The history teacher, **who had a trusty aim with the eraser**, ensured that we never forgot important dates.*
*The car, **which broke down halfway through France**, had to be towed back to England.*
*My new cat, **which somehow jumped on the counter and ate the hot dogs last night**, came home with someone's trout today.*

You don't feel obliged to ask *Which history teacher?*, *Which car?*, *Which cat?* at the end of these sentences. The information given in the subordinate clause is a bonus.

Now consider the difference between these:

The dogs that barked at night did not recognize the thief.	**Restrictive:** Some of the dogs *did* recognize the thief and therefore did not bark.
The dogs, which barked in the nighttime, did not recognize the thief.	**Non-restrictive:** None of the dogs recognized the thief and all of them barked.

Or

I cut down all the trees that were evergreen.	**Restrictive:** Some of them were deciduous and I left them alone.
I cut down all the trees, which were evergreen.	**Non-restrictive:** I've destroyed the entire forest and, by the way, all the trees were evergreen.

In both cases illustrated above, restrictive clauses are introduced by that. Non-restrictive clauses are introduced by the relative pronouns *who, whom, whose,* and *which,* but never by *that.*

It boils down to this: if you can tell what is being discussed without the *which* or *that* clause, use *which*; if you can't, use *that.* Or, as a rule of thumb, if the phrase needs a comma, you probably should use *which.*

Is It Which or That?

Grammarians are divided over whether *which* or *that* should be used in restrictive clauses. While researching this book, we came across all of the following in apparently respectable sources:

> "Many grammarians insist on a distinction without any historical justification."

> "*Which* and *that* are equally acceptable in restrictive relative clauses; *that* is perhaps the less formal of the two."

> "Don't mix *which* clauses with *that* clauses."

It boils down to this: if you can tell what is being discussed without the *which* or *that* clause, use *which*; if you can't, use *that*. Or, as a rule of thumb, if the phrase needs a comma, you probably mean *which*.

A paradoxical mnemonic: use *that* to tell which, and *which* to tell that.

HOW DO YOU PHRASE THAT? (OR, PHRASES)

A **phrase** is a group of words that has either no subject or no predicate, meaning it cannot form a complete sentence on its own. You can have verb phrases (*may sink in gradually*), noun phrases (*grammatical rules*), and adjectival phrases (*even the most complicated*) but until you put them all together (*even the most complicated grammatical rules may sink in gradually*), you don't have a sentence.

Actually there are lots of other kinds of phrases, too:

Participial phrases: *Having to get up in the morning is the worst part of my day.*

Infinitive phrases: *My ambition is to retire by the time I am fifty.*

Adverbial phrases: *I work a long way away, so I need to leave home before my wife.*

Prepositional phrases: *I would love to be able to stay in bed.*

But you don't really have to worry about these technical terms—as long as you remember *to set the alarm.*

4

Punctuation

PUNCTUATION:
THE VIRTUE OF THE BORED?

Author Evelyn Waugh once said that *punctuality* was the virtue of the bored, but he doesn't seem to have said anything witty about punctuation, so we thought we'd just paraphrase him in the title above.

Punctuation can be defined as "the act, practice, or system of using certain standardized marks and signs in writing and printing," and punctuation marks are symbols that are used in sentences and phrases to make their meaning clearer. Those most commonly used in English are the period (.), comma (,), question mark (?), exclamation point (!), semi-colon (;), colon (:), apostrophe ('), and quotation marks (" ").

Cecil Hartley's poem from *Principles of Punctuation* or *The Art of Pointing* (1818) reveals the old-fashioned way that people were advised on how to interpret punctuation when reading sentences out loud.

> The stops point out, with truth, the time of pause
> A sentence doth require at ev'ry clause.
> At ev'ry comma, stop while *one* you count;
> A semicolon, *two* is the amount;
> A colon doth require the time of *three*;
> The period *four*, as learned men agree.

Though it's not a verse that most grammarians would encourage these days, it does give you an idea of the difference between the most common punctuation marks.

> ☛ **Teacher's Corner:** Punctuation existed in Greek texts from at least the fourth century B.C., although Greek and Latin scribes rarely used more than two marks, the equivalent of the period and the comma.

STOP! (OR, PERIODS)

The **period** is the strongest mark of punctuation. It shows its muscle by telling us we need to make a definite pause at the end of a sentence, giving us time to gather our breath or our thoughts, before moving on to the next sentence. Ignore the pause and sentences run together: meaning becomes confused. Periods are also used in (some) abbreviations (see below). They are not used:

- when we end a sentence with another punctuation mark, a question mark or an exclamation point, for example. *Understand? Of course you do!*

- if a sentence ends with an abbreviation. In this case, the period indicating the abbreviation does the job of two: *I have to go out at 9:00 P.M.*

From the Long to the Short of It
An **abbreviation** (from Latin *brevis*, meaning *short*) is a shortened form of a word or phrase that for whatever reason we do not choose

to write out in full. Strictly speaking, an abbreviation is a word or words with the end(s) left off (*Prof.*, *vol.*, *CD*, *VP*), whereas one where something is left out of the middle (*Mr.*, *Dr.*) is a **contraction**, but most people use *abbreviation* indiscriminately to cover both. If an abbreviation of several words forms something that is pronounced as a word in itself (*UNESCO*, *radar*, *scuba*, *AIDS*), this is an **acronym**.

Unlike British English, American English uses the period after contractions such as *Mr.*, *Mrs.*, and *Dr.* Both, however, still use the period for *No.*, *A.M.*, and *P.M.*

A number of common words such as *cello*, *flu*, and *phone* are actually abbreviations or clipped forms (of *violoncello*, *influenza*, and *telephone*) and would once have been written with an apostrophe (or two): *'cello*, *'flu'*, *'phone*. Some people still do this, but most would say it was old-fashioned. Some shortenings have become so accepted that to use the long form of the word would sound pompous:

> *Jane will not be at work today because she thinks she might have* ***influenza***.

> *Tim works out at the* ***gymnasium*** *every day and then catches the* ***omnibus*** *home.*

On the other hand, *stache* instead of *moustache*, *doc* instead of *doctor*, or *gator* instead of *alligator* may be too casual for formal writing.

🖐 **Smart Aleck:** How come the word *abbreviation* is so long?

TAKE A DEEP BREATH
(OR, COMMAS)

"For want of merely a comma, it often occurs
that an axiom appears a paradox."
—Edgar Allan Poe, *"Marginalia"* (1848)

Historically, the **comma** marks a short pause, a place where you
might pause for breath after reading a fragment of text aloud. In
grammar, the comma is used to facilitate meaning by separating
the different elements of a sentence. Some people are comma-
happy; they put commas anywhere and everywhere:

Dear Professor Purvis, [comma, pause for breath]
Please may I have an extra, short, extension on my very late,
and, at this point in time, largely unfinished, English
dissertation?

Other people prefer to leave them out altogether:

Dear Professor Purvis
Please may I have an extra short extension on my very late
and at this point in time largely unfinished English
dissertation?

In the first example, there are so many pauses that it takes forever
to get to the point. In the second, with no pauses at all, we risk
losing the plot. How should we interpret *an extra short extension*?
Is it *an extra, short extension* (that is, a short extension in addition
to the longer extension already granted) or *an extra-short extension*
(an extremely short one, much shorter than the sort of extension

that would usually be requested)? Just a smattering of punctuation would have helped here.

Ha-Ha

My apologies for using this terribly old joke, but it illustrates the point.

A college professor wrote on his blackboard: *a woman without her man is nothing.* He then asked his students to punctuate the sentence. All of the males in the class wrote: *a woman, without her man, is nothing.* All of the females in the class wrote: *a woman: without her, man is nothing.*

So Where Does a Comma Go?

We spent most of our time sitting on the back porch
watching the cows playing Scrabble and reading.

A comma can go in lots of places. Here are seventeen examples:

1. At a place in a sentence where you wish your readers to pause:

    Take a breather, will you?

2. After introductory words or phrases that come before the main clause:

    In the autumn of 1066, the English lost the Battle of Hastings.
    Once upon a time, there lived a boy called Jack.
    Of course, .../However, .../Finally, .../Yes, ...

3. Between separate clauses within a sentence:

In the beginning, when God created the universe, the earth was formless and desolate.

4. Before direct speech:

He asked, "Can you tell me why I should pay attention to these rules?"'

5. In addresses and place names where one part of the place name gives further information about the other:

The White House, 1600 Pennsylvania Ave., Washington, D.C.

The President was assassinated by a gunman in Dallas, Texas (as opposed to any other Dallas).

6. On either side of parenthetical phrases or clauses (those non-restrictive parts that contain extraneous information; see page 139). These are known as paired or parenthetical commas, so there must always be two of them:

She backed up into the traffic barrier, which she could have sworn was not there an hour before, causing considerable damage to her car.

One day in the near future, if we can believe what scientists tell us, this planet will run out of oxygen.

7. After items in a list:

My favorite Victorian novelists are the Brontë sisters, Wilkie Collins, Charles Dickens, and Thomas Hardy.

8. In large numbers. In numbers of more than three digits, use a comma after every third digit (reading from right to left):

I make that 6,000 people.

20,000 leagues under the sea.

The population of Argentina is 34,663,000.

But note that in scientific texts and particularly in tables of figures the comma is sometimes replaced by a space: *6 000, 20 000, 34 663 000.*

9. Around a non-restrictive clause. Be careful with commas here. They change what you mean to say:

I pulled up all the flowers that looked like weeds.	**Restrictive:** I pulled up only the flowers that looked like weeds.
I pulled up all the flowers, which looked like weeds.	**Non-restrictive:** I heartlessly tore all the flowers out of the ground; they also looked like weeds.

10. Before and after an appositive (that's a word or phrase that defines or modifies a noun or pronoun that comes before it):

I, Jane Jones, declare that I was at home on the evening of September 25.

Chérie Blair, wife of former Prime Minister Tony Blair, was accused of not liking cats.

And again, note the difference between:

My upstairs neighbor Bill plays loud music.	There could also be an upstairs neighbor called Ben, for all we know.
My upstairs neighbor, Bill, plays loud music.	Bill is the only upstairs neighbor.

11. Between a dependent clause and an independent clause, where the dependent clause comes first:

    After lunch, my stomach was upset.

    The comma here is optional, but it does indicate (the possibility of) a pause for breath. However, you wouldn't pause for breath in the sentence *My stomach was upset after lunch,* so no comma is necessary.

12. After consecutive adjectives that are equally important in describing a noun:

    In the dreary light of the morning, the rows of gray, pebble-dashed houses, with their unkempt, litter-strewn gardens, failed to inspire tender thoughts of home.

13. In front of conjunctions such as *like, although, but, or, so, and* and *yet* when they are used to link two independent clauses:

    The show was over, but the crowd refused to leave.
    It's going to be a long night, so let's get those coffees in.

14. In place of a word that has been deliberately omitted:

    The room was cold, the bed hard.

15. Before the word *too* when it means *also*:

    Two pairs of ballet shoes and two tutus, too.

    Parenthetical commas can also add emphasis to the word *too* if it appears in the middle of a sentence:

    He'd never really thought about where to put commas in a sentence, but then, too, he'd never thought much about punctuation at all.

16. To emphasize an adverb:

I wrote it down, quickly, which is why I went to the wrong address.

17. After greetings and before closings in letters:

Dear Sir,

Sincerely,

This used to be a hard-and-fast rule, but it is beginning to fall out of favor. Now the hard-and-fast rule is *be consistent:* if you use a comma after *Dear Sir,* use one after *Sincerely,* too.

> ☛ **See Me after Class:** *I find writing English essays really difficult, I'm sure everyone finds that inspiration does not always come instantly, I think you'll find that is so.*
>
> These could be treated as three distinct sentences, separated by periods; or they could be clauses, separated by semicolons. Or, in informal writing, if you wanted to make them sound a bit breathless, you could use dashes. But, sorry, the commas here are just wrong wrong wrong.

Are you feeling tired? Bored? Confused? Let's move on to something more straightforward.

The Serial Comma

The Oxford, Harvard, or serial comma is placed before the final *and, or,* or *nor* in a list of more than two elements. (The names are derived from the Oxford University Press and Harvard University Press, both advocates of this usage.) In British English, it is mostly used to avoid ambiguity, but it is more often used in American English.

He introduced me to Mr. Brown, his teacher and his friend. (He introduced me to one person, Mr. Brown, who happened to be both his teacher and his friend.)

He introduced me to Mr. Brown, his teacher, and his friend. (He introduced me to two people: his unnamed friend and a teacher, whose name was Mr. Brown. Or indeed, if the speaker is particularly grammatically unaware, to three people: Mr. Brown, plus the teacher of either Mr. Brown or the speaker, plus a friend of the teacher, Mr. Brown or the speaker.)

Serial commas are particularly useful if one of the items in a list already contains the word *and,* or in sentences such as this one, where the items of the list are a complicated collection of phrases or clauses. Dick King-Smith's novel *Poppet* contains this perfect example: "He asked beetles and grubs and worms and caterpillars and little lizards and small frogs, and some replied jokily and some replied angrily and some didn't answer."

WHAT IS THIS, THE SPANISH INQUISITION? (OR, QUESTION MARKS)

'To whom, then, must I dedicate my wonderful, surprising and interesting adventures? to whom dare I reveal my private opinion of my nearest relations? the secret thoughts of my dearest friends? my own hopes, fears, reflections and dislikes? Nobody!'
—Frances Burney

Question: When do you use a **question mark**?
Answer: At the end of a direct question.

Well, we'd probably better go into just a little more detail.

Direct questions are things such as:

Where were you when I needed you?
When did you last see your father?
Who's the best team this year?

Indirect questions are things such as:

I wonder who's kissing her now.
I didn't hear what he said.
I know where you are coming from.

These sentences aren't questions, they are statements: *I wonder, I didn't hear, I know,* so they don't need a question mark.

Rule: A direct question needs a ?; an indirect question does not.

Hint: To spot an indirect question, look out for the words *ask* or *wonder,* often followed by *if.*

A question in the form of a statement, known as an **embedded question**, also doesn't require a question mark: *The question whether children learn enough grammar remains to be answered.*

Hint: Look out for the words *whether* or *if*—they often indicate embedded questions.

But *The question is, "Do today's children learn enough grammar?"* The opening words plus the comma have set the scene for direct speech, and the direct speech takes the form of a direct question. So—yes, you've guessed, go to the head of the class—it needs a question mark.

Note: One *asks* a question.
"How much does it cost?" he said. ☒
"How much?" he asked/inquired/questioned. ☑

Rhetorical questions—questions to which we do not expect an answer—are still questions and deserve to end with a question mark: *How much longer must our people endure this injustice?*

Question upon Question

Sometimes a question will be followed with a series of brief questions. When that happens, especially when the brief questions are more or less follow-up questions to the main one, the little questions can begin with a lower-case letter and end with a question mark. Both of the following are correct:

Who is responsible for this? The boy who cheated? The girl who told? Or the teacher who left the answers on her desk?

Who is responsible for this? the boy? Sarah? or Mrs. Dean, who was out smoking a cigarette in the middle of the exam?

But, as so often when there are alternative ways of doing things, you should decide which style you are going to use and use it consistently.

Rule: Do not put a period after a sentence that ends with a question mark. But when a question ends with an abbreviation, end the abbreviation with a period and then add the question mark. *Do you mean 3:00 P.M. or 3:00 A.M.?*

Are You Questioning My Orders?

When a question is really an instruction, use a period instead of a question mark.

Would you take these books back to the library for me?	A polite request. Is it convenient for you to do this?
Would you take back the books as I asked you to do yesterday.	An order. You'd better or else.

SOMETHING TO SHOUT ABOUT (OR, EXCLAMATION MARKS)

"Cut out all these exclamation points.
An exclamation point is like laughing at
your own joke."
—F. Scott Fitzgerald, quoted in *Beloved Infidel* (1958)

The **exclamation point** may be used at the end of a sentence in the place of a period, in order to express strong emotion, such as excitement, delight, fear, anger, or surprise.

Hey!	*Watch out!*
Boo!	*Stop!*
Woohoo!	*Run!*
Wow!	*Fire!*
Ouch!	*Detention! Now!*

They may also be used to catch the reader's attention. Compare:

> *Slow workmen in road.*
> *Slow! Workmen in road.*
> *Elephants please stay in your car.*
> *Elephants! Please stay in your car.*

But beware of overkill. Too many exclamation points make writing overheated. There are no real rules about using them, except *Please restrain yourself.* If you overdo it—

> *I'd love to! Thank you so much for asking! I'll be there in plenty of time! Oh, I'm so excited!*
>
> *I'll kill you!!!!!!*
>
> *Get out!!!!!*
>
> *It tastes disgusting!!!!!*

—you lose the impact that a single, well-placed exclamation point might have. A well-written sentence should be able to pack its own punch. Besides which, exclamation points are visually distracting and can get really annoying!!!!

Rule: An exclamation point ends a sentence in place of a period and should be followed by a capital letter.

☞ **See Me after Class:**
"You won't give me detention, will you?!"
"What is the meaning of this '?!'"

(**Answer: An interrobang**. In formal writing, don't use a
question mark in combination with other marks.)

TWO DOTS
(OR, COLONS)

Rule: A **colon** informs the reader that what follows sums up or
explains what has come before.

For example, it may be used to link two main clauses, where the
second clause explains the first.

> *She was delighted to have the offer accepted: It was the third
> time she had bid on the house.*

Or to introduce a list of items (or, indeed, an example):

> *The cake contained ingredients found lying in the back of the
> kitchen cupboard: flour, baking soda, dried orange peel,
> sultanas, raisins, brown sugar, nutmeg, cinnamon, and mixed
> spices. To this, we just added some milk and an egg from the
> fridge.*

> *You will need: strong footwear, waterproof clothing, a change of
> clothes, high-energy snacks, a small first-aid kit, a good map,
> and a flashlight.*

SUPERCOMMA TO THE RESCUE (OR, SEMICOLONS)

"There were pears and apples, clustered high in blooming
pyramids; there were bunches of grapes, made, in the
shopkeepers' benevolence, to dangle from conspicuous
hooks, that people's mouths might water gratis as they
passed; there were piles of filberts, mossy and brown,
recalling, in their fragrance, ancient walks among the
woods, and pleasant shufflings ankle deep through
withered leaves; there were Norfolk Biffins, squat and
swarthy, setting off the yellow of the oranges and lemons,
and, in the great compactness of their juicy persons,
urgently entreating and beseeching to be carried home in
paper bags and eaten after dinner."
—Charles Dickens, *A Christmas Carol*

Now fighting a losing battle against the less elegant dash (see page
150), the **semicolon** connects two or more independent clauses that
don't *quite* justify being sentences in their own right. It often replaces
and or *but*. It may be helpful to think of it as a "supercomma."

I have tickets for the U.S. Open tomorrow. I bet it rains.	These two short sentences read a bit jerkily.
I have tickets for the U.S. Open tomorrow but I bet it rains.	A little clumsy.
I have tickets for the U.S. Open tomorrow; I bet it rains.	Much better!

Rule 1: You must have a finite clause sentence (see page 125) on
both sides of the semicolon.

Rule 2: Semicolons are followed by a lower-case letter, unless the word in question is a proper noun. A semicolon is also used instead of a comma to break up items in a long and complicated list, particularly when the list has plenty of commas in it already, as in the Dickens quote above.

DASH AWAY ALL
(OR, DASHES)

A **dash** (—) is a horizontal line that may be used alone, or as a pair in place of brackets. It introduces an aside, an interruption, or an additional piece of information, indicates a sudden change of emotion or thought, or shows that words have been omitted at the end of a sentence that has been broken off.

He had said that he would marry her when he got his next promotion—and she, poor girl, believed him.

She—poor girl—believed him.

After hours of careful preparation the experiment actually worked—eureka!

They want that contract—which means they get that contract—by the end of today.

He is an excellent employee, but—

A dash can also indicate that we are carrying on where we left off: *—as I was telling you, I wouldn't be seen dead in a ditch with her.*

Nowadays, dashes are riding roughshod over the poor old semi-colon (*I have tickets for the U.S. Open tomorrow—I bet it rains*), and this is becoming more acceptable, especially in informal writing.

Americans use the longer em-dash (—) and no spaces, while British English usually uses an en-dash (–) with a space on either side of it.

A dash also sometimes takes the place of letters in order to "disguise" curse words (does this really fool anybody?). In this case, the closed-up em-dash, or something longer, is usual on both sides of the Atlantic:

That man who hit me was a real b——d.
Oh, s——.

✌ **Smart Aleck:** An en-dash is named for the width of a typesetter's *n* key. The longer em-dash is the width of a typesetter's *m* key.

JOINED-UP WRITING (OR, HYPHENS)

"A knave, a rascal, an eater of broken meats, a base proud, shallow, beggarly, three-suited, hundred-pound, filthy-worsted-stocking knave; a lily-livered, action-taking, whoreson glass-gazing super serviceable finical rogue, one-trunk-inheriting slave."
—William Shakespeare, *King Lear*

A **hyphen** looks like a short dash but isn't used in the same way. Its function is to join two or more words to show that they belong to each other, and also to separate syllables when necessary—for example, when a word is split in half at the end of a line of type. Hyphens are rather going out of fashion these days, particularly in American English, but they are often useful (and sometimes essential) in clarifying meaning, as the examples below illustrate.

Hang glider pilots in training today.

He wore a new dress shirt and jacket to the dinner.

Fox hunting supporters.

It was a long overdue visit.

They were speaking a nonnative language.

Thirteen year-old boys take placement exams here tomorrow.

She went through it with a fine tooth-comb.

In the above examples, common sense tells us where a hyphen would have been useful. (*Fine-toothed comb*, please!)

Some hyphen rules:

- Be careful with compound adjectives. Hyphenating these incorrectly, or not hyphenating them at all, can cause confusion because we don't know which words go together: *Thirteen-year-old* boys take placement exams; *thirteen year-old boys* would be far too young, and are an unlucky number anyway.

- A hyphen is unnecessary if other punctuation makes the meaning clear without it:

    The old English teacher droned on and on.

    The Old English teacher droned on and on.

    The fact that the word old is capitalized in the second sentence makes all the difference: in the first sentence we know that the teacher is old; in the second, it is the English that is old.

The usefulness of the hyphen in forming compounds that serve as adjectives before nouns is demonstrated in the entries ill- ajd well-.

Example: *She wore a well-tailored suit.*

But the hyphen is omitted when the words follow the noun they modify: The suit was well tailored.

"QUOTATION MARKS"

> "'You are old, Father William," the young man said,
> 'And your hair has become very white;
> And yet you incessantly stand on your head—
> Do you think, at your age, it is right?'"
> —Lewis Carroll, *You Are Old, Father William*

Rule: In direct speech (when we write the actual words that are spoken) we need quotation marks. These may be single or double. Both are correct, in some instances although if you quote within speech, use single within double: *"I find the government's 'nanny state' attitude really irritating," he said.*

Another rule: Punctuation goes inside the closing quotation mark:

> *"Punctuation goes inside the closing quotation mark," I said.*
>
> *"Where did you say the punctuation should go?" he asked for the umpteenth time.*
>
> *"Inside the inverted comma!" I snapped.*

If the spoken words end the sentence, there is no need for extra punctuation:

He asked, "Is this the end?"
They replied, "This is the end."
She screamed, "Help!"

Note that in such a sentence as *"Can anybody hear me?" she yelled.* there is no capital letter after the question mark, because it is all the same sentence despite all that punctuation.

Something to Report?

Rule: Do not use quotation marks for **indirect** (or **reported**) **speech**.

They say that you can't have too much of a good thing.
He asked me how to use a comma.

WHAT'S ALL THE FUSS?
(OR, APOSTROPHES)

The **apostrophe** (') is probably the most misunderstood piece of punctuation we have. At its simplest, it is used to show possession (*his master's voice*) or omission (*you wouldn't dare*). But, of course, it isn't as simple as that.

Thoughts on *Ain't*

"A*in't* ain't a word, so you ain't going to
find it in no dictionary."

✳

"Ignorant people think it is the noise which fighting cats
make that is so aggravating, but it ain't so; it is
the sickening grammar that they use."
—Mark Twain

Leave It Out, Will You?

Rule: When you omit a letter or letters in a word, you should replace it/them with an apostrophe.

If you choose to write *can't* instead of *cannot, we've been here before* rather than *we have been...,* '*or 80s* instead of *1980s,,* you need to replace the missing letters with an apostrophe. Note that the apostrophe in *'80s* tells us that something is missing from the *front* of the word, but it is still an apostrophe. Do not reverse the apostrophe and write *'80s.* And if you write *rock 'n' roll rather* than *rock and roll,* you need apostrophes before and after the *n.*

> ☛ **Teacher's Corner:** The ancient Greeks invented the rhetorical device *apostrephein* (meaning "to turn away"). This had nothing to do with grammar. It described the moment when a speaker turned away from the audience to address a usually absent person or a thing personified—" O Liberty, what things are done in thy name!" This is still known as *apostrophe* today. However, over time, the word's meaning has widened to include "something missing," such as letters and sounds.

Common contractions requiring an apostrophe include:

aren't	*hadn't*	*they're*
can't	*hasn't*	*they've*
couldn't	*isn't*	*weren't*
didn't	*it's**	*won't*
don't	*shouldn't*	*wouldn't*

Such contractions aren't normally used in formal writing, unless someone's speaking, but in a friendly book such as this one they're OK. But remember—the apostrophe is replacing a missing letter, so please put it in the right place.

> "There ain't nothing more to write about, and I am rotten glad of it, because if I'd a' knowed what a trouble it was to make a book I wouldn't a' tackled it, and I ain't agoing to no more."
> —Mark Twain, *The Adventures of Huckleberry Finn*

WHAT'S NOT IN A NAME?
(OR, POSSESSIVE APOSTROPHES)

At one time in the history of the English language, a common way of indicating that something belonged to someone was to add the suffix *-es*.

---

*But only when it's short for *it is*. See page 67.

Singular	Possessive singular
mann	*mannes*
James	*Jameses*

At some point, however, people omitted to pronounce and write the *es*. So instead of an *e* we gained an apostrophe.

The man's hand.

James's book.

This use of apostrophes to indicate possession caught on. In fact, people started adding them to any old word, whether they carried the suffix -*es* or not.

Rule: The apostrophe is placed at the end of a noun to indicate that something belongs to someone or something. It replaces the word *of* in a sentence. If the noun is singular, add *'s*. If the noun is plural, just add the apostrophe.

The boss's chair is for the boss only.	The chair **of the boss**
The animals' feed is insufficient to last the winter.	The feed **of the animals**

Another rule: In the singular the apostrophe is always on the left of its *s*; in the plural it is usually on the right.

The school's rules (one school)

The schools' rules (two or more schools)

The princess's slippers (one princess)

The princesses' slippers (more than one princess)

What the Heck Do I Do with That Apostrophe?

There are—of course—**exceptions** to the apostrophe rules. These are they:

1. When the plural doesn't end in *s*, add an apostrophe followed by an *s*:

   *The **children's** party*
   *The **mice's** lack of eyesight*

2. Names ending in an *s* should be followed by *'s* if singular and *-es'* if plural:

   ***Charles's** last name was Dickens.*
   *Charles **Dickens's** novels are well loved.*
   *The **Joneses'** standards weren't worth keeping up with.*

   Our old friend euphony (see page 94) also crops up here: the moment the word becomes a mouthful, you stop adding an *s*. So:

   *St. **Agnes's** Church*
   ***Jesus's** sandals*
   but ***Barabbas'** criminal record*

3. If the last syllable is pronounced *-iz* or *-eeze*, stick to *s'*, don't add the extra *s*—***Sophocles'** plays*—although, with longer words, it's often easier to paraphrase:

   The inventions of Archimedes rather than Archimedes' (or *Archimedes's*) *inventions.*
   The odyssey of Odysseus rather than Odysseus' (or *Odysseus's*) *odyssey.*

   It also sounds better—and makes you less likely to spit at the person you are speaking to.

4. Then there are organizations that have simply decided that they are above having to employ correct grammar:

   Diners Club International and Walgreens, for instance.

There appears to be no logic to this, but presumably an organization has the right to choose how to spell its own name. That said, ten out of ten for *Macy's, McDonald's,* and *Bloomingdales.*

But Who Really Care's?

The problem is that, in the course of the last few decades, lots of people have become confused about this and—rather than, as they fear, looking ignorant by leaving the apostrophes out—they have started putting apostrophes in places they shouldn't. This is often called the **greengrocer's apostrophe**.

APPLE'S HERE! FREE BANANA'S! FAIR DEAL'S!
NO DOG'S!

Free Margarita's before 7:00 P.M.

But free Margarita's what? You could write *Free Margarita's lover before 7:00 P.M.,* if you wanted him to get out of the office in time to go to the movies. However, assuming that Margarita is an alcoholic drink, there is no need for a possessive apostrophe in either of these examples.

Similarly *VPs, GIs, and the 1970s* don't need apostrophes, unless they are followed by a possessive or attribute. *An* (individual) *VP's expenses,* (all) *GIs' uniform requirements. A 1970s' trend* would belong to the whole decade; *1970's music* is specifically music from the year 1970.

Conclusion: Using an apostrophe in a plural that is not a possessive form is to be frowned on. No if's, and's, or but's.

To avoid confusion, it is permissible—but not necessarily necessary—to include an apostrophe in:

do's and don'ts
the three R's
There are two s's in that word
dotting one's i's
Minding your p's and q's

But in all of these cases, it is a matter of personal taste, and the apostrophe is included only for ease of reading.

The Typo Hunt

Jeff Deck of Somerville, Massachusetts, and his friend Benjamin Herson of Virginia Beach, Virginia, decided they had seen one too many signs with misspelled words.

Armed with chalk and adhesive letters, the duo, who called themselves the Typo Eradication Advancement League, set out in 2008 on a nationwide search to stamp out grammatical errors. After correcting a misplaced comma and apostrophe on a sign in Grand Canyon National Park, they were arrested and charged with conspiracy to vandalize a historic marker. They were ordered to pay restitution and were banned for one year from national parks.

Yours, Mine, and Ours

Rule: The personal pronouns *yours, theirs, its, his, hers* and *ours* never need an apostrophe.

> *The **boys'** burgers, but the burgers are **theirs**.*
> *The **girl's** cakes but the cakes are **hers**.*

The only possessive personal pronoun that needs an apostrophe is *one's*. However, be careful when using it. *One's well* could mean either *one is well* or *the well that one owns*—though with a bit of luck, the context will help you work out which!

> ✋ **Smart Aleck:** We also use an apostrophe in possessive indefinite pronouns: *Is that someone's idea of a joke? That's anyone's guess.*

What Happens When Two People Own Something?

Rule: An apostrophe is placed after the second name when the possession belongs to two people who are mentioned in the same sentence: *Jane and Peter's dog*, not *Jane's and Peter's dog*.

That one is easy because you only have to add *'s*. If, however, you—yes, you—co-owned Jane's dog, you would have to say *Jane's and my dog*, because you can't say *Jane and my's* nor, God forbid, *Jane and I's*.

> ✋ **Smart Aleck:** Achilles heel is the Achilles heel here. Neither Achilles heel nor Achilles tendon has an apostrophe.

And Finally...

Useful mnemonics for remembering the difference between a plural form and a singular form in need of a possessive apostrophe.

Rose's are red
Violet's are blue
Which color underwear
Belongs to these two?

Got that? Oh good. Because we're exhausted.

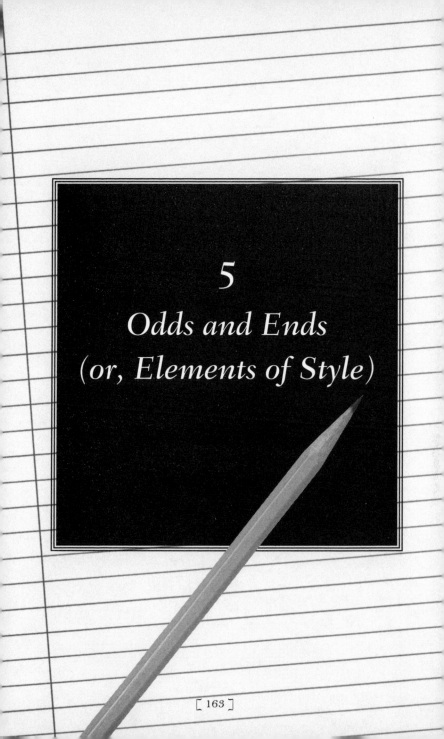

5

Odds and Ends
(or, Elements of Style)

Being a Bit Fancy

There's more to grammar than knowing the difference between a dangling conjunction, a subordinate object, and a non-restrictive apostrophe. So this chapter rounds up a few other points that sometimes cause bafflement.

A Big No-No
(or, Double Negatives)

> "…nor your name is not Master Cesario;
> nor this is not my nose neither."
> —Shakespeare, *Twelfth Night*

Double negatives may not have mattered to Shakespeare, but they do matter in standard modern English.

Rule: Two negatives equal a positive and therefore negate each other. If you want to be negative, use only one.

Sometimes a double negative is obvious—

*I did**n't** do **nothing** right*

*I did**n't** **never** do well in that*

– while others are more elusive:

*His essay **scarcely** needs **no** correction*

*There is**n't** **nowhere** I'd rather be than here with you.*

They are all equally wrong.

> ☛ **See Me after Class:** *I ain't never heard of no one by no name like that.*
>
> On the other hand, when Al Jolson said, "Wait a minute, you ain't heard nothin' yet." in *The Jazz Singer* in 1927, he made movie history.

Yes-Yes to No-Nos

Double negatives are permissible—indeed, useful—when they convey cunning nuances of meaning:

*It was a **not un**usual reaction for someone who has been given bad news.*	Sounds more sympathetic than *It was a usual reaction.*
*I would**n't** say I do**n't** like your new house.*	I am too polite to admit that I hate it.

And they are allowed for emphasis when they belong to different phrases or clauses:

*I will **not** give up, **not** now, **not** ever.*

*You do**n't** ask for much, **no** more than the rest of them, anyhow.*

Positive or Negative?

Interpretation of a **deliberate double negative** may depend on context and intonation.

*She's **not un**attractive.*	This may mean that she is not ugly, but neither is she beautiful—she's not **un**attractive. On the other hand, we may be leaping to the lady's defense—she's **not** unattractive!
*Your visits are **not in**frequent.*	You could visit more often—or you visit regularly enough.
*I **can't not** come if you're singing.*	I don't want to come but I'm obliged to if you are singing—or I wouldn't miss your singing for the world.
*That's **not bad.***	That's good—or it could be better.

Sometimes double negatives contradict themselves to make positive statements:

I'm not not doing my job!	I *am* doing my job!
*There is**n't** a day when I **don't** think about him.*	I think about him every day.
*He **cannot** just do **nothing**.*	He doesn't understand the concept of idleness.

Ha-Ha

A linguistics professor was lecturing to his class.

"In English," he said, "a double negative forms a positive. In some languages, such as Russian, a double negative is still a negative. However, there is no language wherein a double positive can form a negative."

"Yeah, right," said a voice in the back of the room.

Pleonasm, Prolixity, and Tautology (or, Wordiness)

Wordiness—also known as long-windedness, pleonasm, prolixity, redundancy, verboseness, verbosity, windiness, wordage, verbiage, garrulousness, redundancy, tautology, or logorrhoea—is to be avoided at all costs.

"Vigorous writing is concise. A sentence should contain no unnecessary words, a paragraph no unnecessary sentences, for the same reason that a drawing should have no unnecessary lines and a machine no unnecessary parts. This requires not that the writer make all his sentences short, or that he avoid all detail and treat his subjects only in outline, but that every word tell."

—William Strunk Jr., *The Elements of Style*

Imagine what Mr. Strunk would have had to say about either of these examples:

As the firemen climbed up the steps of the ladder to reach the people trapped in the building that was on fire (people with no escape!), the piercing sound of a shrill cry could be audibly heard from up high on the rooftop. Above the loud roar of the burning flames, we heard a woman screaming out at the top of her voice to the rescuing fireman. We sighed a sigh of relief when they finally reached her and she was brought down.

This quarter, we are presently focusing with determination on an all-new, innovative integrated methodology and framework for rapid expansion of customer-oriented external programs designed and developed to bring the company's consumer-first paradigm shift into the marketplace as quickly as possible.

Rule: Be clear; be concise; be simple.

Some Thoughts on Pomposity

"We must have a better word than 'prefabricated.'
Why not 'ready-made?'"
—Winston Churchill

❋

"His speeches left the impression of an army of
pompous phrases moving over the landscape
in search of an idea."
—U.S. politician William McAdoo
about President Warren Harding

❋

"Speak properly, and in as few words as you can,
but always plainly; for the end of speech
is not ostentation, but to be understood."
—William Penn

❋

"Clutter is the disease of American writing.
We are a society strangling in unnecessary words,
circular constructions, pompous frills,
and meaningless jargon."
—William Zinsser

A Waste of Space

Try not to punctuate your speech (and certainly don't litter your writing) with **verbal apologies** such as *and that sort of thing, as it were, do you know what I mean?, to all intents and purposes, needless to say.* Nine times out of ten, they will add nothing. Mark Twain had it right when he said, "Substitute 'damn' every time you're inclined to write 'very'; your editor will delete it and the writing will be just as it should be." The same applies to these empty phrases.

Many of us also diminish powerful words by using them in a trivial way. What we mean is, don't use *awfully, fearfully, terribly,* or *horribly* when you mean *very.* In formal writing, keep these words for when they are needed: *He was horribly scarred by the accident.*

Er, Um, Room for Improvement

Recent research concludes that English speakers use a meaningless word about every nine seconds and that 10 percent of English speech consists of **filler words**. And, um, you know, if you don't mind our saying so, it's sort of boring to listen to.

Rule: If it is possible to cut out a word, do so.

It's Déjà-Vu All Over Again...

Tautological phrases or synonyms (words that mean the same) simply repeat a meaning with different words. Making free with these weakens your writing and suggests that you don't know what the words mean. Our pet peeves are *safe haven* (what other kind of haven is there?) and *PIN number* (what do people think the *N* stands for?) but we seem to be fighting a losing battle on these two. However, there are lots of other nonsenses against which we can still fight:

absolute certainty	*factual information*	*honest truth*
accidental mistake	*fall down*	*new innovation*
added bonus	*fictional story*	*stupid idiot*
awful tragedy	*final conclusion*	*sum total*
climb up	*free gift*	*terrible disaster*
close scrutiny	*grab hold*	*true fact*
complete opposite	*end result*	*unconfirmed rumor*
8:00 P.M. in the evening	*HIV virus*	*variety of different*

✍ **Smart Aleck:** How come *needless to say* is always
followed by something being said?

Note: One particularly common misuse is of the word *unique*.
Unique, from the Latin for *one*, means "being the only one of a
kind; without parallel." So it is (just about) possible for something
to be *almost unique* (that is, there might be two of them, whatever
they are) but not for it to be *quite unique* or *very unique*.

"It was a sudden and unexpected surprise."
—BBC correspondent

✳

"Every Superbowl is totally unique—and
this one is just the same."
—Young football athlete

Let Me Repeat Myself
Not all **repetition** is bad. The repetition of key words, phrases
and sentence patterns is obviously important in poetry.

It was many and many a year ago,
In a kingdom by the sea,
That a maiden there lived whom you may know
By the name of ANNABEL LEE;
And this maiden she lived with no other thought
Than to love and be loved by me.
I was a child and she was a child,
In this kingdom by the sea;

> But we loved with a love that was more than love—
> I and my Annabel Lee;
> With a love that the winged seraphs of heaven
> Coveted her and me.
> —Edgar Allan Poe, *Annabel Lee*

And it can be effective in prose too:

> "She turned towards me immediately.
> The easy elegance of every movement of
> her limbs and body as soon as she
> began to advance from the
> far end of the room, set me in a flutter
> of expectation to see her face clearly.
> She left the window—and I said to myself,
> *The lady is dark.* She moved forward
> a few steps—and I said to myself, *The lady is young.*
> She approached nearer—and I said
> to myself (with a sense of surprise which
> words fail me to express), *The lady is ugly!"*
> —Wilkie Collins, *The Woman in White*

Of course, as with all good things in life, this can be taken to extremes:

> *If one doctor doctors another doctor does the doctor who
> doctors the doctor doctor the doctor the way the doctor he is
> doctoring doctors? Or does the doctor doctor the way the
> doctor who doctors doctors?*

Say That Again

A word that has two meanings that are the opposite of each other is called an **antagonym** or **contranym**.

> *That horse will **bolt** unless you **bolt** the stable door.*
>
> *The soldier was **bound** for home, when they caught him and **bound** him.*
>
> *Having **clipped** off his baby hair, she **clipped** the pieces in his baby book.*
>
> *We escaped from the mudflats as **fast** as we could, before we were stuck **fast**.*

These examples are all grammatically correct, every word is used accurately, but they still manage to sound silly. It's best to avoid them.

☝ **Smart Aleck:** What's another word for *thesaurus?*

Choose Your Words Carefully

As we said earlier, English is full of easily confused, similar-sounding words, with plenty of opportunity for deliberate puns and inadvertent verbal gaffes.

Visiting relatives can be boring.	Are they visiting you or are you visiting them?
I had been driving for forty years when I fell asleep at the wheel and had an accident.	No wonder, I expect you were rather tired.
Q: *What gear were you in at the moment of the impact?*	A: Gucci sweats and Reeboks.

Yogi Berra was a master of this form of miscommunication—"He hits from both sides of the plate. He's amphibious."—but while not many of us would aspire to his heights, he is an object lesson in what can happen if you don't watch what you say. On the other hand, you can have a lot of fun with words if you don't mind what you say. See what we mean?

Enjoy These Other Reader's Digest Best-Sellers

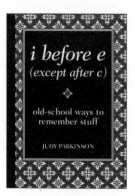

Featuring all the memory-jogging tips you'll ever need to know, this fun little book will help you recall hundreds of important facts using simple, easy-to-remember mnemonics from your school days.

$14.95 hardcover
ISBN 978–0–7621–0917–3

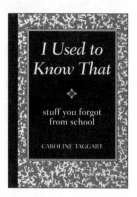

Make learning fun again with these light-hearted pages that are packed with important theories, phrases, and those long-forgotten "rules" you once learned in school.

$14.95 hardcover
ISBN 978–0–7621–0995–1

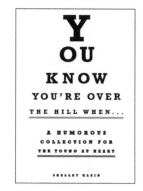

This laugh-out-loud collection of heartwarming jokes, quips, and truisms about the joys of aging will keep you entertained for hours.

$14.95 hardcover
ISBN 978–1–60652–025–3